Wandering Along The Himalayan Foothills & Beyond

A Veteran's Travelogue

Wandering Along The Himalayan Foothills & Beyond

A Veteran's Travelogue

Colonel Mani K. Gahatraj (Retd)

Vij Books India Pvt Ltd

New Delhi (India)

Published by

Vij Books India Pvt Ltd
2/19, Ansari Road, Darya Ganj
New Delhi - 110002
Phones: 91-11- 43596460, 47340674
Fax: 91-11-47340674
e-mail : vijbooks@rediffmail.com
web : www.vijbooks.com

© 2015, Author

First Published : 2015

ISBN : 978-93-82652-90-8

ISBN ebook : 978-93-82652-91-5

Price : ₹ 395.00

This book is a collection of various travelogues undertaken by the author.

Printed & bound in India

"A good traveler has no fixed plans and is not intent on arriving."

– Lao Tzu

Contents

Foreword

This book presents a traveler's very personal experiences as he walks along the marked or unmarked trails of the Himalayan foothills crossing hills and valleys, quenching thirst from a fresh water mountain stream, watching in silence the ripples of a placid lake or a waterfall splintering into millions of particles over rocks, enjoying the feel of mountain breeze, smiling at strangers, clicking children on way to school or stroking the neck of a village dog that follows him. In other words the author shares the thoughts that cross the inner recess of his mind as he walks along, takes turns, rests, befriends strangers, drinks a hot mug of tea along the trail and just celebrates fresh dew drops dangling from a pink rose petal in a village garden.

Having known Mani for half of my life of seven decades, I have seen him growing from a young man in to a very young old man!! He has always been an explorer at heart, be it exploring his potential as a die hard soldier or exploring his inner spiritual world, I have seen him passing through all these realms with the same cheerful smile and a twinkle in the eyes. So I was not at all surprised when he took up to trekking and exploring the mountains but what surprised me most was his travelogues. I was not aware of his lucid writings, a true gift of God and I am indeed impressed with what I read. Here I am not talking just about the smoothly flowing language or expressive narration but his keen observation, his empathy and his love for the surrounding; be it a playful child on the roadside, a tail wagging dog, a lazy mountain stream or a quiet sunset over the hill tops, his writing caresses them all with a loving gaze and brings them alive to the reader. What I find most enjoyable in Mani's travelogues is that he takes the reader along the trail and helps her or him to experience every bend and scent of the trail while the writer himself takes a back seat to the places and people, which is a great quality for a travelogue writer.

Reading between the lines of Mani's travelogues one also experiences his deep love for mother nature and a clever comparison of the days of placid life of yore in the hills and the present turmoil of degradation of nature and environment while leaving subtle hints about the need to conserve nature. Understanding that the wheel of time cannot be rolled back, this travelogue endeavours to take the readers to a peek view of the factual or visualised past world so as to help them understand and appreciate this world towards better preservation.

Col Mani Gahatraj deserves kudos for bringing out this very interesting collection of his travelogues which I am sure is going to be a source of pleasure to many nature lovers across the globe. I wish him a very happy and healthy life in years to come and many more years of travelling and writing for the reading pleasure of millions of people.

Jaipur   Veena Shivpuri

25 Sep 2014

Acknowledgments

World moves in strange ways making events happen in unimaginable and unpredictable characteristics. In 1985, when I was posted near Gurdaspur as the logistics staff officer of a brigade least did I fathom that two people there would be the cause and effect of this book. First was my boss Brigadier Hira Ballabh Kala (Now a retired Lieutenant General). Our friendship started with common love for books and developed into a beautiful bond that lasts till date. He also introduced me to bird watching, gardening & star gazing. When General Kala found that I was struggling to write articles he encouraged and gave me confidence to keep writing, telling me that whatever form one can write, is a divine blessings. He has been the real inspiration behind this book instilling in me the confidence that I could scrawl my thoughts and produce this book, thank you sir. The next man in Gurdaspur was Major (now retired Brigadier) PK Vij, the operational staff officer in a neighbouring brigade and also from the Assam regiment as me. After all these years, he is the one publishing this book. Thank you PK for your encouragement and for taking the burden of publication hunting off my shoulders. I also thank Veena Kaul Shivpuri, my regimental sister for her lifelong support, encouragements and valuable advise on this book. I thank Kalpana Pradhan McGrath for finding time during her short holidays to proof read the Kalimpong article and render valuable inputs. Finally, I thank Kodak Kalimpong for sharing their valuable old photos.

In loving memory of my father, Pratap Singh Gahatraj (24 Jan 1900-26 June 1986) whose journey to Lhasa in a mule caravan in the mid 1920s followed by four years of adventurous life in Tibet, planted the seed of travel in me.

This book is dedicated to

My mother, Budh Maya Gahatraj (1910-1949)

&

My eldest sister, Shanti Lata Gahatraj Ranpal, who brought me up as a second mother and whose love, care, patience, guidance, encouragement and slaps, made me the person I am. She continues to inspire and encourage me to this day.

"Twenty years from now you will be more disappointed by the things you did not do than by the ones you did, throw off the bow lines, sail away from the safe harbour, catch the trade wind in your sails, explore, dream, discover".

– Mark Twain

Khecheopalri: the Holy Lake of West Sikkim

"Bizarre travel plans are dancing lessons from God"
– Kurt Vonnegut

The Lake at Dawn

Life form in the lake along with the bog, marsh and the jungle hill that envelope it, is slowly stirring back to life. As the morning rays of the rising sun, filtering through pine and juniper jungle, touch the highest spires of coniferous hills and start dancing on the surface of this 3500 years old lake it is time to witness the beauty. At 5 am, it is the dawn of October morning at Khecheopalri Lake in West Sikkim in India. Tucked away in a corner of the mountain; hidden by the surrounding jungle and unseen from outside, this holy water body is located at an altitude of 1700 meters (5,600 feet) as a little bowl in the middle of mountain jungle. The crisp morning air has a whiff of approaching winter and though smug and comfortable in a warm jacket, I savor the morning chill brushing through my face. Walking the short distance from the Trekker's Hut, across 100 meter long Tsozo Village market I see few doors opening and early morning smoke puffing through roof tops of few houses, perhaps brewing the morning tea for early risers. Day is just breaking and the world here is still semi dark and silent. As I cross the small clear water stream, over a culvert and continue walking along a narrow cobbled footpath that meanders into the woods I find myself entering into a different world of nature and its silence. Sound of crickets, frogs, insects and occasional chirping of birds greet me. The stone path spirals like a tunnel through juniper and pine trees across giant ferns bowing down towards the footpath as if greeting visitors to the lake. Along the slope of the path there are roughly chiseled rocks with painted prayers written in Tibetan scripts.

Path to the Lake

The tunnel opens to a clearing and the cobbled path spreads out to a wide area with rows and rows of colorful prayer flags hung like canopy between the trees. Towards the end of this canopy, some 50 meters away, I see a small log chapel like structure standing on rough stone masonry foundation covered by green tin roof with corners curved skyward in a typical oriental architectural design. Such a place is called *Cheykhim* in Tibetan/Sikkimese for a small chapel like place of worship where devotees light *Cheymi* (butter lamp) and pray. A rough conical stone masonry, chimney that looks like an incinerator stands in front of the chapel, a trail of smoke rising lazily above its conical tip. This structure is hollow inside like a chimney with an opening to place the herbs, *Sang* and incense sticks. It is called *Sangboom* and there is unique fragrance of holy essence from the burnt *sang* which, in this case, are the green leaves of pine tree and pine cones that catch fire rapidly.

2

The Canopy of Prayer Flags

As I enter the holy sanctum of *Cheykhim* the chapel, I see rows of lighted butter lamps, *Cheymi* places on a platform meant for the purpose. Opposite wall has a platform that is adorned with stone and metal statuettes of Lord Buddha, Guru Padmasambhava, Maa Tara and Lord Shiva and *Trishul* (three pronged javelin, weapon of Lord Shiva for destroying evil). Above the platform are the framed photos of *Rinpoche* (incarnate) Buddhist Lamas (monks). A young lama is lighting *Cheymi* and an elderly Hindu Priest is chanting *Mantras* in low whispers in front of Lord Shiva's statue. It is a silent coexistence of two religions in peace and harmony.

"Cheymi" the butter lamps

3

Cheykhim & Sangboom

Standing in the midst of the solitude of raw nature in complete sync with spirituality of the holy place, I am awed by the mesmerising site of the Khecheopalri Lake with its turquoise blue water. The water surface, that reflects the jungle hill like a mirror, is placid except for few ripples caused by the unseen breeze. Towards the far side, at the bottom of a thickly wooded hill, the lake is surrounded by tall grasses beyond which jungle line envelops the entire lake. Just below and towards the left of the *Cheykhim* and *Sangboom* the flat area steps down to another path that leads to the approach of the lake in the form of wooden jetty with green tin roof extending across the marsh to the edge of the water body. The jetty has rows of prayer wheels on both the sides. I remove shoes and walk towards the other end, turning the rows of prayer wheels on my right. The belief is, when the wheels turn; prayers written on it are expressed to the cosmos and taken by the wind to Dewachen, the abode of Gods, a silent concept of prayers. At the jetty's end I stand and look at the lake in its silent existence. The only sound is that of the nature such as the rustle of leaves, call of a bird or croaking of frogs. The lake is surrounded, firstly; by a ring of bog with tall grass and shrub over wet and marshy ground, thereafter the pine and poplar jungle takes over as the land start rising to meet the ring of hills beyond. The shape of the lake is elongated that would roughly represent the shape of a huge giant feet. Hindus believe it to be the foot print of Lord Shiva whereas Buddhists believe that the footprint is that of Goddess Tara. As I stand holding the railings of the jetty and experience the placid lake there is a faint sound of water splashing and I see a pool of catfish surfacing and moving around rapidly. I am told later by the locals that they are attracted by the vibrations of the approaching footfalls on the wooden jetty and the sound of rolling prayer wheels. I saw huge pool of these fish swimming around and literally looking up towards me.

Morning Mist before Sunrise

However, as I learn later, the surfacing is also for the attractions of food thrown by few tourists to see more of these fish on the surface, an act forbidden by the law of the lake. I wish people would understand that God and nature provide food for all living beings in their natural habitat and that there is no need to disturb the harmonious balance of nature. Fish must be left to eat their own natural food that is in abundance in the lake as such throwing food into water, besides disturbing the habitat also pollutes the environment. Wishing to have a feel of the holy water I slip out of a gap in the railing bars and lower myself down to the wet bog next to the jetty. My naked feet touch the wet, cold and soft marshy surface and I step on few scattered stones, barks and dry wood to reach the edge of the water. Bending down I scoop the holy water, put it on my head and drink some. The water is pleasantly warm and sweet to taste. There are rows of colorful prayer flags and *Khadas* (silk scarf for holy offering) hung across the shrubs and small trees around and a prominent iron *Trishul* with red scarves tied around it standing on the water edge. I tie up two *Khadas* around the branch balancing myself on a small stone so as not to sink my feet into the wet marsh. Having completed the small venture I retreat my steps back to the jetty and stand there in silence savoring the lake. If there was no time bound world one could live with such a beauty forever. As the sun starts climbing up the Easter sky shortening the shadows I kneel and bow down in reverence to the lake touching the cold wet wooden planks of the jetty with my forehead. It is time to leave, albeit reluctantly, I walk back slowly while turning the prayer wheels to my right. After wearing shoes I take the stone cobbled path back and sit on the wooden bench next to Cheykhim facing the lake and savor the moment with the holy lake. In front of me, amongst the tall grassland over the bog area there are numerous small, about 6 to 8 inches diameter spider webs with dew drops hanging and dripping through its fine woven threads. The antenna like webs are mysteriously facing at an angle towards the western sky like an array of futuristic antenna discs receiving and transmitting communication with the outer space. Such a well arranged symmetrically placed tiny spider webs in the marsh could only be a well designed system of the wild, unknown to man.

Sitting by the lake I am glad to be the only human in the area and the only sound are the rustle of the jungle, croaking of frogs and crickets punctuated by occasional whistle of Myna and twitting and chirping of red tailed minla, broad billed warbler chestnut breasted partridge, hoary throated browning, yellow vented warbler, fluttering of noisy sparrows, and hammerings of "woody" the woodpecker. The jungle around is rich with bird life as this lake is also the transit camp for the Trans Himalayan migratory cranes. Amazingly, the lake surface is always clean, devoid of fallen leaves of the jungle around. It is believed that birds seem to have taken upon themselves the task of cleaning and keeping the surface of the lake clean by industriously picking up leaves fallen on the surface. It is only here that such a strange and interesting phenomenon exists that birds pick up the leaves as soon as it falls on the water surface. The locals also say that if lucky and blessed ones could sight a pair of elegant white swan swimming on the far side of the lake. As the morning advances towards day it is time to leave before the noisy tourists would start pouring in by 9 am and the silence of the lake would give way to the daily grind of human encroachment.

The Jetty

Spread over an area around 9/10 acres the lake is fed by 2 perennial and 5 seasonal monsoon streams and has only one outlet. It is about 20 to 30 feet in depth and home to multitude of fish such as carp and Garra etc. Since fishing is not permitted the numbers of fish are increasing at a steady speed.

It was mid October in West Sikkim with winter just around the corner. Compared to the heat and dust of Siliguri, It was refreshingly cold and I felt a pleasant sense of warmth in my cotton cargo pant, dawn jacket and woolen skull cap to top. Sitting on the bench next to the chapel, I gaze at the lake and soak into the pleasant experience with the raw nature, listening to tweeting and chirping of birds, croaking of frogs, humming of bees and sounds of insects. This is a wish fulfilling lake and I wish and pray for peace and good health of all sentient beings and, selfishly, for the success of my writings and continuance of travelling, trekking and golfing for all times to come, amen.

As the sun rays start dancing over the lake surface and human habitation little far away stirs to the morning life, it is time to leave before the peace and tranquility of the lake is disturbed by the noisy tourists.

Before leaving I pay homage to the deities of the lake by burning incense sticks in the Sangboom and watch its smoke drift slowly upward from the chimney opening and dissipate away in the wilderness of the pine jungle. I walk back slowly along the cobbled path still unable to take my eyes off the emerald lake. I reach the small bridge across a clear water stream outlet of the lake and cross it to reach a small courtyard of a mini village boutique that sells Buddhist artifacts by a young Japanese lady married to a local Lepcha boy Nima. I had befriended the couple during the spring of 2011 when I had stayed in their home stay on top of the hill overlooking the lake. Nima told me candidly about their love life that blossomed into nuptial. He was a guide taking tourists to the high Himalayas and it was during one of such treks she was a tourist, they met, fell in love and made history in this small Western Sikkim Village. After spending few years in Japan they are back home; he continues as a tourist guide and she runs this humble boutique living happily ever after. God bless them. As I chat with her Nima comes along with a plate of yellow fried rice and steaming mug of tea for his little Japanese wife. We shook hands and he rushes out to fetch me a hot mug of tea that I welcomed and enjoyed with a big thank you, *Thusi Che.*

Back to the Trekker's Hut, a sumptuous breakfast of millet bread and cottage cheese curry with generous amount of fresh green chilly was waiting for me. I savored the food and washed it down with another hot mug of salty Sikkimese tea. After breakfast I walked around the small village bazaar that is dotted with tea shops, lodges and general stores that sell ration provisions, Buddhist artifacts, chips and aerated drinks. At the end of the bazaar just before the path leading to the lake is a sign board that describes the legendary history of the lake, courtesy Government of Sikkim.

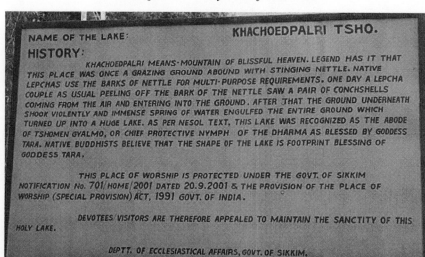

NAME OF THE LAKE: **KHACHOEDPALRI TSHO.**

HISTORY:

KHACHOEDPALRI MEANS-MOUNTAIN OF BLISSFUL HEAVEN. LEGEND HAS IT THAT THIS PLACE WAS ONCE A GRAZING GROUND ABOUND WITH STINGING NETTLE. NATIVE LEPCHAS USE THE BARKS OF NETTLE FOR MULTI-PURPOSE REQUIREMENTS. ONE DAY A LEPCHA COUPLE AS USUAL PEELING OFF THE BARK OF THE NETTLE SAW A PAIR OF CONCHSHELLS COMING FROM THE AIR AND ENTERING INTO THE GROUND. AFTER THAT THE GROUND UNDERNEATH SHOOK VIOLENTLY AND IMMENSE SPRING OF WATER ENGULFED THE ENTIRE GROUND WHICH TURNED UP INTO A HUGE LAKE. AS PER NESOL TEXT, THIS LAKE WAS RECOGNIZED AS THE ABODE OF TSHOMEN GYALMO, OR CHIEF PROTECTIVE NYMPH OF THE DHARMA AS BLESSED BY GODDESS TARA. NATIVE BUDDHISTS BELIEVE THAT THE SHAPE OF THE LAKE IS FOOTPRINT BLESSING OF GODDESS TARA.

THIS PLACE OF WORSHIP IS PROTECTED UNDER THE GOVT. OF SIKKIM NOTIFICATION No. 701/HOME/2001 DATED 20.9.2001 & THE PROVISION OF THE PLACE OF WORSHIP (SPECIAL PROVISION) ACT, 1991 GOVT. OF INDIA.

DEVOTEES/VISITORS ARE THEREFORE APPEALED TO MAINTAIN THE SANCTITY OF THIS HOLY LAKE.

DEPTT. OF ECCLESIASTICAL AFFAIRS, GOVT. OF SIKKIM.

Sign Board of the Lake History

Siliguri, the Base to the Hills: Travelers to Darjeeling, Sikkim and Bhutan reach Siliguri from all over the world, by air from Delhi, Kolkata and Guwahati and by train from the same major destinations. People from Bhutan, Nepal and Bangladesh reach by road. Siliguri, an old and ever expanding city, is a major business and communication centre of North Bengal and acts as gateway to the hills of Sikkim and Darjeeling and the Kingdom of Bhutan. This city is expanding on all fronts towards its final destination of being the metro of the East next only to Kolkata. There is no major industry but it is major a trading centre and a communication hub towards the Hills of Darjeeling, Sikkim, North East, Nepal, Bhutan and Bangladesh. There are already two major Malls, Cosmos and City Centre and more are mushrooming. With major multispecialty hospitals the city is also the Medical centre for the people of the hills that still lack major health care institutions.

On the flip side, in spite of visible efforts by the city municipality, Siliguri is also the city of open drains, poor garbage disposal system, unauthorized shanties and horrible traffic that is at the mercy of 8 seater noisy and very reckless diesel driven auto rickshaws and multitudes of cycle rickshaws. As per Siliguri Wikipedia, the city has 16,000 cycle rickshaws licensed by the municipal corporation and an additional 55,000 illegal ones that ply on its already congested roads making it a driver's nightmare. Roads have been broadened only to make way for parking for more vehicles. The only river

Mahanadi that flows through the city, instead of being an oasis of peace and serenity, is squalor of filth that people living in the vicinity use its shore as open latrine and garbage dump. Unimaginable now but during the 50s my brother and I used to swim in this river that had clean water rumbling down from the hills. Sadly now the river is dry during winter and monsoon comes mercifully to wash away the filth only to deposit more dirt and silt on its banks. Notwithstanding the filth and congestion, the city boasts of sleek residential areas such as North City, Uttarayon and Barsana (outside the city) and many high end complexes in Punjabi Para, Parnami Mandir and ESCON Mandir roads and more are mushrooming. There are reasonable hotels and restaurants and three multiplexes to boot. With political disturbance in the hills during the last decade, many public schools are making forays into Siliguri and doing good business.

Siliguri has very nice eating places and my favorites are *Punjabi Kadai* and *Sartaj* for sumptuous Indian bill of fare and *Sagar* for vegetarian and south Indian dishes. My favorites are mutton keema and tandoori *laccha parathas* in Punjabi Kadai and tandoori roti and chicken curry and malai kofta in Sartaj. Even Bidhan market houses age old Bengali culture based small eating places such as Kalpana Pice Hotel, Kalpatru Pice Hotel that serve very tasty and authentic Bengali rice and fish curry called *Chital Peti* the taste as well as the price are awesome. There is a very famous and authentic Bengali Dhaba named *Bedween*, located just behind the Auto Rickshaw stand that serves good mughlai dishes such as Biryani, Kebabs, Roomali roti, parathas, rolls etc. There are dozens of wayside *Momo* shops but unfortunately there is no worthwhile Chinese restaurant. The only one called *Taiwah* does provide sort of Chinese food but the service, system and the attitude is an apology. Outside the city there are authentic Tibetan and Nepali restaurant serving good Tibetan and Nepali dishes in Salugura, Salbari and Sukna.

For impulse shopping of all types of Chinese goods there are Honkong Market in Bidhan market area and Golden Plaza along Burdwan Road (opposite Howrah Petrol Pump). For varieties of apparel and linen items at wholesale and reasonable rates Seth Srilal and Bidhan Market are best. When one is around these areas it is worthwhile to step in to Kolkata Sweets near Vegetable Market for best Bengali sweets with special reference to *Rasmalai*. Places worth visiting which are ISKON Temple, Buddhist Monastery in Salugura, Savin Kingdom for children, Madhuban Park in Military Cantonment in Sukna, Surya Sen Park and Mahanada Wild Life Sanctuary in Sukna.

Drive to Khecheopalri

Siliguri to Pelling in West Sikkim is 131 kms and takes approximately 3 hours for straight drive. Needless to mention that the drive is subjected to imponderables like traffic snarl, road repairs and broadening work, tea and meal breaks. As such it is safe to plan approx 4 hours for the drive. Pelling to Khecheopalri is 32 kms and takes about an hour's drive along a graveled road. As usual the condition of road from Siliguri to the lake can best be described as "the good, the bad and the ugly". Last year at a chance meeting a MLA from Jorthang told me that this West Sikkim road is being turned into a four lane highway, insallah.

Road from Siliguri to Sevoke is a smooth broad 2 lane highway (NH 31) that knifes through the neat Sevoke Military Cantonment and Sevoke Forest. From Sevoke Bazaar to Coronation Bridge (3 kms) is another smooth, well carpeted road snaking along he mountain curves running almost parallel to Teesta River. This road is adorned with good highway signs; however, unfortunately this stretch is marred by delays due to railway gate blockage and heavy traffic from/to North East, Dooars, Sikkim and Kalimpong. From Coronation Bridge to Teesta Bridge near Teesta bazar (37km) NH 31is forever in the making and subject to traffic jams & delays caused by repairs and expansion; as such, it can be dusty and slushy depending on the season. There are good stretches passing through refreshingly green forest areas and the meandering Teesta River keeping company all along. There is definitely a strong case for a major flyover across the Sevoke railway crossing. The entire stretch of this road is dotted with small bazaars where one can stop by for tasty Nepali ethnic meals or masala tea in Bihari tea stalls. One can even buy home grown mushrooms packed in plastic bags in Rambi Bazaar. This road meanders along the hill almost in tandem with Teesta River and at places the precarious road sides drop dangerously to the fast flowing river. I wish the highway authorities would see some sense in building proper side barriers to stop unfortunate vehicles from falling off as that has been the case many a times with loss of precious lives. For the drivers there is need for cautious driving, not to speed and dead slow in curves. The good part is the view of the river all along the drive is fantastic. From Teesta Bridge to Chitrey is 2 kms from where road to Kalimpong branches off to the right and we continue along NH 31 for another 3 kms to Melli Bridge. From Melli the road to West Sikkim branch off as we cross another bridge over Teesta where as NH 31 continues towards Gangtok. From Melli bridge to Jorthang in

West Sikkim (68 kms) the state highway is narrower but good. One can halt at Jorthang for lunch in Nepali, Bhutia or Marwari/Bihari restaurants or tea or snacks in one of the fast food joints. Jorthang to Pelling (49 Kms) the state highway continues along the river as also starts climbing up towards Geyzing, the Distt Headquarter of West Sikkim. After Geyzing we cross the famous Pemayangtse monastry located opposite Mt Pendim Hotel of Sikkim State Tourism and then drive down hill for another 3 kms to Pelling, the ever expanding tourist destination hub of West Sikkim with hotels and restaurants mushrooming and multiplying. As I see Pelling is another concrete jungle in making. Having started from Siliguri leisurely (a mistake) at 10 am, by the time we reached Pelling it was 6 pm and dark. However, with the aim of visiting the lake early morning in its natural glory and beauty, we pushed the Bolero across another 26 kms of graveled road with scanty habitation and reached the lake side Trekker's Lodge at 8 pm. Had it not been for the delays due to traffic jams and road blocks we would have taken about 7-8 hours and reached by 5-6 pm as against our delayed drive of 10 hours. Next time I shall definitely start at 6 am and reach Kheolpalri between 3-4 pm to celebrate the holy lake in peace both during sun set and sun rise. "Early bird catches the worm" but then "Early worm is eaten by the bird"

Bird Life in the Lake

During my earlier visits during 80s and 90s the lake area was enriched by varieties of birdlife. Those days, sometimes during early morning sneak view, I have been able to identify some beautiful water birds in the lake area such as large cormorant, little cormorant, common teal, tufted duck and have also observed with great pleasure dash of the White-breasted water hen and moorhen dashing across the footpath into the marsh bushes. The lake also used to be a resting-place for Trans-Himalayan migratory birds such as bar headed goose and cranes. Sometimes during earlier winter visits I have been fortunate to hear forests resound to full-throated bird-song of variety and richness. I am delighted by the sight of drongo, nick named *Kotwal* (police) by the famous ornithologist, Salim Ali, based on its characteristics of chasing away crows from the nests of other birds as it tries to steal their eggs and chicks. It is, however, the whistling tune of the Himalayan Whistling Thrush which is pleasantly familiar sound in this area as also along the rivers and streams in this part of the world. Himalayan forests are the home of some of the most colorful birds such as pheasants, the cock Monal that even rivals the peacock in colorful splendor. This time, sadly, I did not see many of these exotic birds sighted during earlier visits but I hope and pray that some of them are still around in spite of invasion by the human kind in terms of encroachment, tree felling, over grazing, fire wood collection and above all, material and noise pollution by environment unfriendly tourism. This is one reason I drive straight to the lake area even if it is late night, stay in a modest room in the Trekker's hut and visit the lake early morning so as to be with the holy lake in its natural environment of birds and bees.

Trek to Sandakpu – Phalut

"Once you have travelled, the voyage never ends but it is played out over and over again in the quietest chambers. The mind can never break off from the journey".

– Pat Conroy

On the March –Between Sandakpu & Phalut

24 May 2013 – Siliguri to Maneybhanjyang, the Base Camp

The cell phone alarm went off, it seems, at the set time of 4 am but I did not hear, obviously the effect of couple of pegs of Haig's the previous night, so to say to herald my long awaited trek to the illusive Sandakpu-Phalut of my life. I forced myself out of the bed and did my morning dos starting with a cup of tea with the wife and later a sumptuous breakfast of 4 *paranthas* and vegetable curry I left in an auto rickshaw, called by my wife, for Darjeeling motor stand. I bought both the front seats to be comfortable. The tariff was INR 160.00 per seat so it was cool.

The road from Siliguri to Sukna, 20 kms is good and traffic in the morning is ok and not so crowded. From Sukna Military Camp to Simulbari, 5 kms, is also well maintained with quite few speed breaker humps, kind curtsey army, but the freshly carpeted road to Kurseong via Raney is a beauty, at least for the time being, hopefully it will withstand the onslaught of the monsoon. Hitting Kurseong just in one hour and half we drove on towards

Darjeeling. Weather also playing up with cool overcast sky but no rains, the drive along the NH 34 meandering between pine forests was a breeze. It was good to get the whiff of aromatic pine trees after a long time. The drive was enjoyable till Ghoom; highest Railway station in the world till Lhasa took the cake away few years back. After Ghoom the usual traffic snarl started. I am amazed at the thousands of Sumos, Boleros, Scorpios, Maruti vans fully loaded with tourists, mostly from Kolkata and rest of W. Bengal. It is difficult to understand that Darjeeling being so crowded with buildings and multitude of people, not so organized waste disposal, scarcity of water, expensive hotels and not so certain political environment that causes instant strikes and shutdowns of traffic, continues to attract tourists nonstop. I contribute this to two possible factors; first, the brand name Darjeeling that is as old as Darjeeling itself and second Bengalis love for the hills. I found it only during this trek, befriending a group of 5 of middle aged Bengali entrepreneurs from Kolkata. They told me very candidly that their lot just love the hills specially the Himalayas and would like to visit the hills again and again. I have also understood that Bengalis are the most travel loving people of this nation and I am certain that they form the major bulk of tourists of the country. Also the good parts of them travel with family members from grandparents to grandchildren. Touring is a passion for them and that is good news.

Darjeeling will always be Darjeeling the international brand, well known all over the world, thanks to the British rulers who saw the depth of the place in respect of its location atop the hill, altitude of 7000 ft and the cool climate, as also the fact it was then a great vantage point to see and enjoy the views of the Himalayan ranges that included the Kanchenchunga and the Everest. Today much of the beauty is lost due to rapid escalation of the concrete jungle, population explosion and the inversely proportionate buildup of matching civic amenities. This process is further accentuated by the disturbance caused by political turmoil laced with avoidable violence during long periods of 80s and 90s. Although the sense of violence commenced as response to the deployment of Paramilitary Forces and its insensitivity towards the local population, unfortunately, it snowballed into a long and violent battle of supremacy between the new power brokers and those who opposed it. Resultantly, locals were hurting the locals completely loosing site of their vision and mission. Sad but true for one of the most beautiful spots on planet earth. We only hope that old beauty and glory of Darjeeling will one day return to its original glory & pride. Else it will only become folklore of the distant future signified by concrete jungle and accompanying multitudes and unmanageable dirt. It is time to wake up and take action towards restoring Darjeeling to its old glory and beauty, whether Gorkhaland or Switzerland.

Back to track, a quick cuppa tea at one of the motor stand restaurants and I was rumbling on a Sumo towards Maneybhanjyang, again full front seat. To get the real feel of a back packer, I had decided to travel like one instead of using my new Bolero. I found it comfortable to buy the whole front seat at reasonable rates. Drive back towards Batasia, Jalapahar and Ghoom was eventless but as the road takes a turn towards North West for Maneybhanjyang via Teensukhia, once again the Sumo meanders along the curves of the road between the pine forests and occasional road side hamlets. Taking off from Darjeeling at about 12.30 pm, we reached Maneybhanjyang via Sukheypokhari by 2 pm. As advised by the driver of the Sumo, I got down at the office of "Society of Highlander Guides & Porters Welfare Association" located at the entrance of the town. The office had a huge wall poster of the Singalila National Park trek route with details of the routes, distances and important vantage points or resting places along the road. The office guy briefed me in details about trekking, transportation and en-route accommodations. I learnt that it was necessary to take a guide cum porter. There were options to travel by the local Land Rover or trek or make use of both along selective points along the route. On my request he fixed up a guide cum porter for me to be used from the next day that is 25th May 2013. It turned out that Bejoy Chhetri would be my companion, friend and guide for the next 4 days.

It was also a blessing that Bejoy is a very nice, kind, affable fellow with deep knowledge of the land and its flora & Fauna. It was a pleasure to be in his company. He talked when he had to and answered my numerous queries about the land, treks, flora and fauna; he also knew when I was too tired to talk and kept the rhythm of the walk with me. As we were marching along the high altitude from Sandakpu to Phalut, he guided me along the walkable shortcuts leaving the jeepable track not so far away. He showed me the boundary pillars between Nepal and India and places where the track had been passing through Nepal. When asked as to how there was no habitation in such a vast area he told me that Government had taken steps to clear the entire Singalila National park of habitation. He said that there were, till recent past some dwellings in the forest. These people kept cows and yaks and supplied milk, curd, cottage cheese to the nearby villages.

I spent the evening walking around the small bazaar of Maneybhanjyang. I learnt that the Indo-Nepal border passes through this small town. I walked across towards Nepal side in search of STD booth since I found none on the Indian side. I came across a nice Nepali restaurant, very homely that one could sit inside the house and eat. I asked for a cup of tea checking that I did not want powder milk, I was pleasantly surprised by a very nice cup of strong tea made of handmade tea leaves. I made my calls, had tea as also bought half a kg of handmade tea @ 180 and left. It started drizzling so I went into my hotel "Kanchenchunga" and rested. Dinner was noodle soup called "Thukpa". It was a blessing in disguise that next day, 25th May was Buddha Purnima and meat was not being used. I have always believed in following vegetarian diet and remaining teetotaler during travels of any kind. Precautions are better than cure!!

Next morning got up early, got ready, prayed and went to another restaurant close by that served chapatti and vegetable curry. After breakfast I walked over to the Land Rover Association office. Upon discussion with these people it made sense to go up to Sandakpu by Land Rover and then commence trekking from there onwards. So a Land Rover was fixed @ INR 3800 for drop to Sandakpu. If I wish to halt enroute I would have to pay extra INR 500. Bijay, the guide arrived on time. We rumbled off from Maneybhanjyang at about 8.30 am in a black 1954 vintage Land Rover that had seen better days but it was geared up and well maintained to take on the tough and steep gradient graveled/stone road of the high altitude. At the exit point I had to buy an entry ticket @ INR 100 from the Forest Check point and they checked that every person who entered the Singalila National Park had a guide along. That is one of the systems engrained to ensure that no untoward incident took place along the not so hospitable terrain ahead. The system of guide and Land Rover also provided the much needed local employment. There are about 80 plus guides cum porters and 60 plus Land Rovers. I think this is the only area where the old mountain horse Land Rover still plies with ease. I am happy that the roads to Sandakpu and Phalut or left rough, stony with very sharp turns and steep gradient. For if it is turned into a smooth black top road we will find all the vehicles of the world converging in these parts with the resultant pollution and traffic snarls and accidents along the way as the collateral damage.

As we drove up, the gradient of the road became steep with frequent sharp turns. Only the local drivers could take on such roads behind the wheel of the Land Rovers. After couple of kilometers we came across an abandoned Travera Wagon along the road. We reached Chitrey and found a massive prayers ceremony was being conducted at the monastery for Buddha Purnima.

Chitrey Gumpa

I bought ghee, biscuits and incense stick packets, went inside the Gompa and offered these and sat down amongst the huge congregation to say my Buddhist Prayers, "OM HA HUNG VAJRA GURU PADMA SIDDHI HUM". Moved on towards Tumling and Tolong and reached Meghma about 3 kms uphill drive from Chitrey. This is a beautiful place, a small hamlet with a new Gompa where Buddha Purnima Puja was in progress. This place being almost along International Boundary with Nepal, people from across the border were also participating in equal number. With the main Puja over, the tradition of carrying the *Poshtak* the holy quatrains, each of several hundred pages held on each side by wooden cover and bound by holy clothes. A procession of villagers from both sides of the border were carrying these holy quatrains on their heads and slowly moving towards a holy "stupa" about 5 kms away. The procession would go around the stupa that has a huge prayer wheel driven by the force of a mountain stream. Finally the procession would return back to the Gompa and place the quatrains back in its place inside the precincts of the Gompa. Like rest of the people present I also stood on line and received blessing by bowing and touching the Holy Quatrains with my forehead. Hot Tea was being served outside the Gompa after which I was guided to the beautiful stone masonry cottage that served as community hall where hot sumptuous vegetarian lunch was being served. This is the place of local politician, Madan Tamang who was killed in Darjeeling few years back.

His family seems to be the main force behind the Puja Programme. RIP Madan Tamang.

Meghma - Buddha Purnima Procession

As I started after this well fed lunch we passed through more people coming from Nepal side. Strangely these people from Nepal, young ladies were dressed up in long maroon top with long green *mangal sutra* like garland cross slung from right shoulder to left waist. The road became rougher and steeper, crossed Tumling without a halt and reached the mist covered Gairaibaas by midday. Had a hot cup of tea at "Magnolia Lodge" and rumbled on.

A rough poster at Tumling showing road direction to Nepal.

Cuppa Tea at Gairibas

Poster on Singalila National Park inside Magnolia Lodge, Gairi Bas

Sandakpu, the Destination, 3636 M (11926 feet)

We drove steadily along the rough stony track, crossing Kalaikata and Kalpokhari, small hamlets with few shops and lodges and finally reached Sandakpu by 2.30 pm.

This magnificent place, the highest in Darjeeling Hills has been a major destination for the nature lovers all over the world. Its beauty lies in its remoteness and out of the world view of major Himalayan Ranges, Everest, Kanchenchunga, Makalu and Lhotse as also the most beautiful sunrise view it provides to the travelers. Although little cloudy and a light drizzle, that blocked the magnificent view of the famous Himalayan ranges but the sheer beauty, greenery and the cool weather of the place mystically covered by the drifting mist, gave enchanting beauty to Sandakpu.

The sturdy Land Rover-1950 Model

Wanting to experience as a true backpacker, there was no accommodation booking in advance. I headed for the PWD guest house where I tried using my ex-army card but it was full. There were two expensive lodges, I decided against Sherpa Chalet, Sunrise Lodge and Namo Buddha Lodges being more expensive than needed and decided to go for the dorm bed in the humble Government Tourism Lodge A. There are 3 of such Govt lodges, A, B & C. Unfortunately C has been raged by fire last winter. These lodges are humble and cheap run by a family of four Sherpa, an elderly couple and their grown up son and daughter. There was a dorm with 20 beds @ 120 INR and 2 rooms of 5 beds each @ 500 INR. 2 Indian type toilets and 2 bath rooms that had seen better days. The dorm and rooms were clean with wooden cots placed very close with hardly any leg space in between let alone a bedside table. I took one bed in the corner and grabbed the only table to place my rucksack. Hot tea was served immediately on asking but the quality needed improvement. After tea I went out for a walk to enjoy the view and beauty of the place. My guide, Bijay took me to a Shiva Temple just across the border in the Nepal side. It was a strange place that seems very old cave at the foot of a very huge deodar tree with many stone formations that resembled Shiva Ling. Clear spring water was flowing from inner side of the rock formations. Not so strange in

21

these parts of the world that the place was worshipped by both Hindus and Buddhists. Many diyas were lighted inside the sanctum sanatorium to mark the Holy Day of Buddha Purnima and an elderly lady who was lighting more Diyas told me that her wish had been granted, God is indeed everywhere in all forms, we only have to have faith. It was a community kind of dinner for all the trekkers, a simple menu of rice, daal (lentil) and potato curry. Tired and hungry as all of us were, we wolfed it down in candle light as there was no electricity. Blissfully even the cellphone communication were off, happily I felt a sense of wilderness and went to sleep. The night temp had come down but a blanket and a quilt were enough.

25 May 2013: I got up early morning by 5 am and walked to the kitchen for a mug of tea, the house lady had just got up and I was the first one to get tea. Although not to my taste of strong and not so milky tea it was hot and enjoyable for the morning cold. There was a little ray of hope as clouds began to clear up and we could see wee bit of shiny *Kanchenchunga* on the eastern horizon. There was a mad scramble to the view point for the view but it was short lived. The clouds rose to hide the majestic mountain. This was also the day I would commence my 21 kms trek to Phalut. So after bath with half a bucket of hot water @ INR 25 and breakfast of hot Chapattis and scrambled eggs with coffee. Total bill for lodging and boarding was INR 475.00. Not bad for a backpacker. It was a good idea to stay at the Trekker's Hut as I was able to mingle and chit chat with other young trekkers. I started at 7 am with guide Bijay in toe carrying my humble and light army rucksack. He showed me Phalut, a distant hill covered by clouds. We followed the rough stony, muddy and partly graveled road that was almost plain. Initial progress was slow with cold and stiff body of 69 years old. But as we progressed slowly and after about 3 kms the body warmed and limbs got limbered up I was almost swinging using my umbrella as the walking stick that was helpful. We trudged on slowly and surely admiring the beauty of the nature and the wilderness. Since Sandakpu is 11926 feet and Phalut is 11800 feet, the general altitude along the track would be around 11000 feet. At this altitude pine and deodar trees are over giving way to only Rhododendron trees and high altitude ferns. In spite of the season for flowering being over by end April even at this time of the year some varieties of Rhododendrons were in bloom and it was indeed magnificent site. The track runs along the ridge line between Sandakpu and Phalut, which from a distance almost resembles a saddle with Sandakpu as the pommel and Phalut as the cantle. However, the track is not all straight as looks on the map. It goes up and down following the mountainous path of valleys and crests.

Camel hump on way to Phalut

Northern most part of the Darjeeling hills and Singalila National Park borders with Ilam district of Nepal. However, even in Nepal side the place is fortunately remote as such not disturbed by the human habitation and subsequent development. I have been told that after declaring the area a National Park, Government has removed few settlers from the forest who practiced dairy farming with cows and yaks. This is indeed a very wise move, for, if allowed to remain, the human population would have naturally multiplied, encroached into the forest and finally destroyed it. As a result, the forest has become very thick and almost impenetrable that provides safe haven to the wild animals and birds. No wonder the area is a paradise for trekkers, a genuine fame that has travelled across the world. Even at this late stage of the season when the monsoon is knocking at these hills I came across and befriended young trekkers from France, Salvia, USA & UK besides the most usual trekkers from Bengal. It is so good to see that middle aged and young people of Bengal have taken to the hills, as it transpired during my discussion with young minds of Bengal they just love the mountains specially the Himalayas. No wonder most of the domestic tourists are from Bengal. I wish more people, young and old would take to trekking and try to understand nature that gives us the basic subsistence of life.

We came across few yaks grazing lazily on the green meadow, probably from Nepal side. I clicked a big bull Yak, it was enormous and looked at me without much interest and continued grazing. Another place I clicked a flock of goats grazing on short bushy plants along the track. They looked healthy

A Lone Yak

with spring in their legs. After about 10 kms we took a break, sat on a fallen tree trunk and rested. I was carrying some ORS sachets and thought it a good idea to pour the contents into the water bottle. We kept drinking few sips after every few kms and derived instant energy while quenching thirst. Now the climbs were getting steeper and tougher and the length of plain track was a welcome relief, not so the descent as it was not very kind to my old knees.

Rhododendrons in bloom

By 11.30 am we reached a small hutment of Forest Post that also served as a resting place for the trekkers. The Forest Guard doubled up as a tea shop owner. As I walked to the old village style kitchen I found the Guard brewing tea for us on the wooden fire of ancient type of mud fire place. With tea we had the "Champa" that I was carrying and that injected a fresh lease of life to my tired body. Tea with yak milk cost @ 20 INR and I bought a mineral water bottle for INR 40.00, very expensive indeed. As we resumed our journey for another 7 kms it started drizzling lightly but threatened to down pour anytime. I must confess that I had not bothered to carry water proof because I find it cumbersome and rather suffocating. All I had against the torrential rain that would be a usual feature in these parts at this time of the year, were an umbrella and Stetson hat. So I prayed that it should not rain. Being a Hindu and a practicing Buddhist I repeatedly chanted the Guru Rimpoche (Padmashamva) mantra.

The Last Lap

The last 3 kms to Phalut was steep climb and although along the well paved stone track it was quite a back breaking task to walk up the 3 steep kms of the 21 kms. However, somehow the extra hidden energy tends to manifest itself that gives us the necessary drive to the last lap of any race. As taught by the Army, during tiring and difficult marches all that was required to be done was to keep putting one leg forward at a time and not look too far ahead as that would only tire me more. Instead it is better to look back and appreciate the distance and the climb one has covered that gives boost and encouragement to move forward. Using all the tricks learnt earlier in life I reached Phalut at 2.10 pm. It took us exactly 7 hrs. 10 mins to trek 21 kms in the altitude of about 11000 feet with about 1 hour break in between. However, more than the timings and reaching the destination, I immensely enjoyed the journey, the nature walk, the wilderness, the yaks and above all the blooming rhododendrons. I must also thank Guru Rinpoche for keeping the rain away from me. This is something of a "believe it or not". Every time it started drizzling and the Mother Nature threatened to rain I prayed to the Guru Rinpoche, "OM AH HUNG VAJRA GURU PADMA SINGH HUM" continuously. So much so that it almost danced in my lips in rhythm with my stepping. Lo and behold, there was no rain. It is also interesting to note that trekkers who were following were drenched to the bone as it started to rain heavily almost immediately after I reached Phalut. Thank you, "Guru Rinpoche".

Phalut after 7 hours Trek across 21 kms.

Phalut has only one Government owned Trekker's Hut that looks nice but abandoned colonial cottage from outside and a ghost house from inside. The rooms were shabby suffering from years of neglect. Kitchen had the ancient wooden fire place for cooking and most part was black with wood fire soot collected over the years. I walked into the kitchen and found couple of people, not tourists, sitting by the fire and chatting, obviously this was the only available place in the huge colonial house that was warm to sit by. I walked in to this warm hearth and announced to the people present in Nepali, "I am 70 year old retired colonel, just arrived after 21 kms trek, how are you guys going to make me comfortable." Immediately there was commotion and everyone got up. The forest Guard got up from the chair and offered me the coveted chair. I asked as to who was who and found out that the person by the fire place was the only care taker of the Trekkers Hut as he proudly told me, "I am from the Tourism Department." Rest were tour guides who had arrived earlier by Land Rover. I asked for a cup of tea and the care taker got busy brewing it in a black kettle, hardened by years of sitting on wooden fire, a cup for me. I learnt that the Tourism guy was the one and only representative of the Government. He was cook, care taker, cleaner, maintenance man, procurement officer, house keeper and overall in-charge of the colonial style lodge. However, the Forest Guard being more elderly as also senior man of the Government with beat post located adjacent to the lodge, was the de-facto boss of the town, specially for the weary guides and porters. When I pulled my rank and age he chickened out of the comfortable chair against the fire and I promptly occupied it.

Two Indian style toilets and two bath rooms strategically located opposite kitchen were pathetic to say the least. Windows broken, no wash basin, no water in the tap and no flush system existed. To wash the cold posteriors and flush down the human excreta, meager water was kept in a dirty half cut plastic jar with a dirty broken mug. The western tourists who are not used to washing their crappy posteriors with water like we Indians do, had thrown the used toilet paper pieces in one corner. In any case Indian style toilets are pretty hard for most of westernized crappers specially for senior citizens whose vintage knees have just creaked 21 kms in high altitude. If I had a choice I would have preferred to do it outside in the jungle but unfortunately there was no big enough bush for the purpose in the near vicinity, besides, I did not want a blood thirsty leech finding its way into my intestines from the wrong side. It started pouring hard and other trekkers trooped in, mostly drenched. Perhaps as a result of pulling rank and age, I was given a huge room with two cots @ INR 125.00. When I tried to move a cot further away from mine I found it was nailed to the wooden floor and boasted of 5th leg for support, perhaps against adventurous couple of yore. Two dirty curtains of questionable color and design were hung on a bamboo stick and when I tried to draw it so as to make the cold room warm it fell down from the pelmet. Windows were rattling against the wind and rain and the bed linen, blanket and quilt were dirty and had definitely seen better days. I am amazed that Singalila National Park, Sandakpu and Phalut are world famous trek areas attracting tourists from all over the world and yet the condition of the one and only Government's Tourist Department Lodge was in such a sorry state of affairs. I have no hesitation to say that such pathetic show and mismanagement of an internationally important Tourist Destination in India is a "National Shame". I have seen in other places in Darjeeling Hills where fashionable monolithic tourist lodges, way side inns and restaurants have been constructed over the last 25 years, however, its upkeep and maintenance is zero and some of the places are either burnt or abandoned. It seems the only purpose of these wasted infrastructures was to benefit the obliging contractor and the connected political masters. Points in question are Pin Tail Village near Panhca Nadi, Siliguri, group of similar type French Villas in Mirik, a way side restaurant in Dudhey and another burnt and abandoned structure near Raney. Ambitious projects that started with a political bang but ended in a whimper. No one in the power corridors of the hills and plains seem to notice such apathy. Hope, they see sense in having an attractive, comfortable and an International standard infrastructure in place and one such thing comes up we hope and pray that it is not overused or misused by the officials. A strict set of Standard Operating and accounting procedures would be the need of the day to be implemented by stricter implementation policy. It is possible. I understand Uttaranchal Government Tourism is guided by such efficiency as they have employed retired service officers in charge of such institutions. Political will is the need of the day. Hopefully such a project will see the light of the day, one day; and to quote the 3 witches of in Macbeth; "When the hurly burly is done and the (political) battle is lost and won", "Fair is foul and foul is fair, hover through the fog and filthy air of (self-serving politics)". Amen.

Dinner was rice, daal and potato vegetable that was undercooked. I saw the cooking was being done by the guide cum porters. The only table and couple of chairs near the fire place were already occupied by the western trekkers so my guide hastily got me a chair by the kitchen fire place. I ate in silence with illumination by kitchen log fire and a small flickering candle. Amen.

It rained the whole night and I had a nice sound sleep under the dirty blanket and quilt, after all 68 years old bones needed good rest and got it. Next morning when I got up by 5 am it was still raining and the place was misty. However, by 7 am it started clearing. One of the guides went to the view point to see if the view of the majestic mountains had cleared. No luck but by then the rain had completely stopped and by 8 am, after breakfast of half cooked chapattis and same potato vegetable I decided to commence marching towards Gorkhey, a downhill distance of 15 kms.

Leaving Phalut for Gorkhey

We started at 8.30 am when it was nice and sunny. The Bengal Group of 5 not so young men in their 40s had already started half an hour back and the Western group were just getting ready. The track was wide and gradual decent, and as we moved along the early morning sunshine that added beauty to the rain fresh forest all around us. Partial view of Kanchenchunga, half hidden by the clouds was still magnificent.

A view from Phalut

On way to Gorkhey-Kanchenchunga covered by clouds

More rhododendrons in full bloom, pink, cherry, white, lavender colors, spreading riot of colors across the jungle, *"a thing of beauty is joy forever"*, so said John Keats. The blooming trees were smaller, almost like bushes. One needs to study the rhododendrons in depth so as to be able to enjoy the beauty of this flower in its entirety.

Rhododendron tunnel

The path was a combination of mule track and foot path and it was passing through varieties of jungle landscape and fauna. We passed through pine forest, then came the small structured bamboo jungle locally called "Mallebu", then came giant sized ferns heralding the path on both sides like a natural decoration to welcome the weary traveler. As we consumed the distance and moved closer towards Gorkhey the path became steeper descent that was not very kind to my old creaking knees. The umbrella stick was a great help and support. We indulged ourselves with quick halts sipping ORS water and passing water.

Blooming Rhododendrons & creaking knees

The last lap to Gorkhey was a knee punishing steep descent over a narrow path that almost sent us in all our fours. Suddenly my heart swelled as I saw the glimpse of Gorkhey. A small village of few scattered tin roof huts interspersed by cultivated fields and cow sheds. I heard loud sound of water rushing downhill. Bijay told me it was Gorkhey Khola (stream).

As we descended downhill and the view of the village became clearer I could see the beautiful Gorkhey Khola meandering down the hill side, dancing along the huge rocks while turning the fresh water into milky frothy broth as it cascaded down hill dividing the village into two halves. The village with a dozen hutments mingled with cowsheds and cultivated fields were surrounded on all sides by green forest of pine trees. The forest extended up to and beyond horizon on all sides. It was heavenly beautiful. I could live here forever or till the end of my natural term of life on this planet. Amen.

At this stage of trek my one and only need was a clean western type commode. I could not imagine punishing my aching knees by bending

A view of Gorkhey below

beyond the limits of its elasticity in an Indian style toilet. Lo and behold, seek and you will find, ask and you shall be given, so said Jesus Christ. Bijay took me to Eden Lodge and much to my pleasant surprise the land lady showed me a small, clean and wall to wall carpeted room with attached toilet. The site of clean western style commode was a dream come true. I took it without second thought. Unlike the Government Lodges in Sandakpu and Phalut, the linen, blanket and quilt were fresh and clean another blessing in the jungle. I requested the young land lady for strong milk tea with ctc tea

A Stream near Gorkhey

leaves, my usual favorite. Tea was hot and tasty, no wonder, the milk was freshly brought from the cowshed.

A bridge to Sikkim at Gorkhey

I removed my hiking shoes and shocks, wore slippers and moved around the area enjoying the tea and the beauty of the nature all around me. A local mastiff came wagging its long furry tail and sat next to me. Great company. I gave him some of my left over biscuits and he wolfed it down happily and looked expectantly at me leaking its mouth signaling for more biscuits. Sunset was another beauty, I sat by the bridge on the stream and drank the raw beauty of nature. We had reached by 2 pm, so lunch was being prepared.

I saw healthy and fresh mustard leaves in the field as also ripe red tomatoes and requested the little landlady if she could cook the same for my lunch as also and make Nepali *chatni* out of garden fresh tomato and chilly. Lunch ready in a jiffy; served to me on the kitchen table that I relished it to the core. "God of Small things" indeed. We look for big deal material happiness but the real happiness can be derived from such joyful moments with nature. After lunch I went for a walk and saw a beautiful bridge that connects Gorkhey village with Sikkim. As the shadows of the pine trees lengthened, and sun went over the horizon of the western pine jungle, few villagers trudged back home after hard days' work in the fields. Mother hen started collecting its small noisy chicks and nudged them moving towards the small thatched shelters in respective homes. Bleating goats were being driven to their respective cages by the house kids. Smoke started drifting from huts heralding the preparation of supper in the warm mud fire places by the

Warm Hearth at Gorkhey

mother of the homes. That was dusk at Gorkhey. After late and sumptuous lunch I did not have much appetite so ate little supper of rice, *daal* and mixed vegetable and went to sleep early. Although nursing tired limbs and aching knees after trekking 36 kms in 2 days I was happy and thrilled to be where I was by choice. I looked forward to a good night's sleep and a hearty crap in the western toilet the next morning. God Bless this cradle of nature, "Gorkhey".

The Last Lap from Gorkhey to Sri Khola

Sunrise in Gorkhey was another beautiful site that started with sunrays brightening the tips of the jungle of pine trees. With previous night's rain the village and the jungle around had become rain fresh. Smoke started puffing from the houses and I could see my land lady taking fodder to her cows. I noticed with joy the baying of the calves asking for mother's milk and goats bleating past to graze in the nearby fields while mother hen protectively guided her chicks to early morning worms. A lone eagle flew over the village sky in anticipation of a careless morning prey. As I walked into the warm kitchen I was greeted by a hot mug of tea, sat in the warm kitchen sipping tea admiring the simple things of life like a warm, glowing kitchen of wooden fire. The simple breakfast was sumptuous bowl of dahlia porridge and 2 boiled eggs washed down with another mug of tea. That as usual also blessed me with a very hearty and full blast exit policy on the much needed "western throne".

34

Sunrise at Gorkhey

We marched off at 8.30 am with Bijay in toe. Across the bridge, along the path the village mastiff was sitting by, perhaps waiting for me to say his goodbye. After giving a not so concerned look at me he trotted off .Goodbye nice dog, I hope to meet you again. Few hundred meters across the village other side of the stream that path suddenly entered into dense jungle, wet and fresh. The path covered by fallen leaves was wet and almost slushy at places systematically decorated by fresh mule or horse dung. I did not find it dirty. The dung was fodder for worms and insects that automatically tend to appear around their food. Well-designed ecological circle of life as some these would

A Dhamma friend –Till we meet again

in turn become food for bigger insects and birds. It was like passing through God created tunnel of forest. There is method in God's madness.

Nature's Bounty near Gorkhey

The climb was short, steep that lasted about 30 minutes. Suddenly we broke into a flat open plateau and the track continued in a gradual upward gradient. I saw the first house of village Samanden. The village was as beautiful as Gorkhey but fewer houses. I was touched by the site of a mare grazing lazily on the lush green lawn of a small home stay cottage. The new born calf was lying contently on the lawn. These are rare sights even in remote areas, one has to be lucky to come across such beauty of nature in a world techno-gizmos.

Another small cottage with magenta pink primrose tree in full bloom. Further along the way there was a beautiful log cabin house, a Forest Trekker's Lodge. I saw very few houses and fewer people a total contrast from the overcrowded hill towns that have abundance of carbon di-oxide. After this village the path passed through pure and fresh jungle of pine trees, shrubs, creepers, streams and more streams.

We kept marching slow and steady as the path gradually descended till we came across the same Gorkhey Khola that had meandered around the hill to find us back on the trail. After this stream the path went up the hill in a steep gradient. We climbed on huffing and puffing, taking sip of ORS mixture to energize ourselves. We reached Ramom, the last village before our final destination for the day, Srikhola. It was again a small village with a school and a newly inaugurated Gompa. The prominent house was Namo Buddha Lodge. It was double storey wooden cottage with GI Sheet roof. The whole balcony and courtyard was full of colorful potted plants spreading riots of color. The flowers were mostly geranium, roses.

Samanden Village

Tired and thirsty after the arduous climb I was ready for a hot cup of tea and snacks. Bijay took me to this lodge and before anything happened I walked in to the kitchen that had warmth of wood fire burning hearth. It seems the man and lady of the house were sitting by the fire and they were jolted by my sudden appearance. Perhaps so because it was quite a well to do place by the local standard and the owners seem to be well off hence the civilized way of surprise at an alien invading the privacy of their kitchen. I announced that I was an

Nature's Gate

Geranium in a Rammam Home .

old and weary traveler and was looking for a hot cup of tea. The man guided me to the drawing room through the connecting door and offered me seat. We got talking and I was made to understand that the family had similar lodges in Sandakpu and Rimbik. Tea was tolerable but hot and on my asking for snack I was offered Champa, the barley powder. I was surprised to find that the house hold did not know how to serve a simple thing like Champa. It is normally mixed with black tea or milk or hot water, pure ghee and sugar or salt to taste. I was offered just the powder in a bowl and expected to make my own cauldron paste. I did and ate. That was hot and filling. Perhaps because of my frank and sweet talk my offer for payment was politely refused. Instead they took my contact details for future reference. Thank you good hosts, God Bless your home.

Rest of the trek was downhill along freshly dug up road alignment that took steep descent. Landslides had started showing up as nature's response to digging mother earth for so called development. At places there were small landslides in progress and we had to run down to avoid being crushed by a falling boulder. More houses appeared on the way down. Upon looking up towards the hill side I could not imagine I had just crossed them with my 1944 vintage body.

A human like stone face along the path.

After painful descent finally we reached Srikhola at 2.30 pm, 6 hours trek, not bad I guess. The place was so deeply tugged into the fold of Srikhola the stream that it was almost invisible till we actually came face to face with the first house that was again a well-designed French Villa style house. I did not wish to go inside. We trudged along to our destination, Goparma Hotel. I had finally finished my ambitious trekking and had done 52 kms in 3 days. Satisfied and tired I threw myself on the first available cot in a small room. Immediately after, it started heavy downpour and I could hear the rumble of Srikhola passing through the side of the hotel, in half asleep half dream state. Went to sleep blissfully.

I had been carrying my military hip thermos filled with Napoleon Brandy all along the trek but had no opportunity to partake it for fear of high altitude sickness that can be degenerated into deadly pulmonary edema. Now was the chance. So when I got up by 7 pm I found nice company as 5 young trekkers from Kolkata had fetched up. I asked them if anybody was in a mood for a drink. They said they were also planning to invite me over to join them for a drink. They had also brought their quota of Antiquity Blue

Tourist Lodge Srikhola

whisky. We trooped into the dining room at ground floor that was connected with the kitchen by a half wall. Snacks had already been arranged by the young enterprising trekkers. We sat around the table and clicked our yera glasses and drank to celebrate the successful completion of trek as the stream flowing adjacent to the guest house, now in torrent with recent rains, rumbled on.

Next day, 28th May, I got up early, went to the kitchen and asked for a hot, strong sweet cup of tea to the sleepy, groggy eyed maid. She obliged and surprisingly it was as good as I wanted. I drank it with half a packet of biscuits so as to have a hearty exit policy. I did it, painfully though on a "*deshi toilet*". By 6.30 am Bijay and I started towards the bridge as that was the rendezvous with the only passenger service sumo. None came. It was drizzling but stayed on at that. I decided to walk and reach a nearby village 2/3 kms away to catch the transport. On the way I found several lodges and a youth hostel. Finally after about 3 kms we reached a small wayside hotel. Waited there for half an hour and finally got into the sumo that came along. Although I had booked a front seat the young boisterous driver told me to take the second seat. I said nothing doing and got into the first seat. A middle aged man got in at another small village stop and asked me as to my caste, I told him my caste is human being and did he have a problem with that or did he find a suitable groom in me for his daughter. He shut up for the rest of the journey till he got down meekly at Sukheypokhari. The driver was a cellphone freak. He would not leave talking on the phone even in sharpest of bends with one slip and we would be diving down free fall. He would look ahead, steer the vehicle at the same time punch number for another call. It was endless. I decided to keep quiet and kept on with my prayer bid. Another stop, a man was getting in and he shouted at the driver as to why he had not kept the front seat. Looked like this guy was a local boss kind of a man as the driver told him that the front seat was his only but this passenger has occupied it. That guy said, "Who" most menacingly. As the driver pointed towards me I gave a cool unconcerned look to the void and kept on with my prayer beads. Nothing happened and we drove on at the deadly hands of this cellphone freak. At Sukheypokhari I drew cash from the one and only ATM of SBI and gave Bijay a well-deserved hefty tip and in turn he bid me goodbye with Khada and hug. I reached Darjeeling by 11 am. Now that there was no Bijay I carried my rucksack and walked towards Siliguri motor stand. Lo and behold, I was home 2.30 pm sharp to the delicious chicken curry lunch laid out by my wife. I showered changed into clean clothes for a change and ate a hearty lunch downing it with a bottle of beer. Rina asked me if I was going to shave. I told her I would do so only after I finish pounding the lap top with this travelogue. Now that I have done so, I shall shave tomorrow morning before heading for early morning golf at Sukna Army Golf Course. Cheers!!

Taksang Gompa: A Holy Trek in Bhutan

"We shall eventually get to love the mountain for the very fact that she has forced the utmost out of us, lifted us just for one precious moment high above our ordinary life, and shown us beauty of an austerity, power and purity we should never have known if we had not faced the mountain squarely and battled strongly with her."

- Francis Young husband

Taksang Gompa (10,240 Ft.) Paro, Bhutan, a view from the valley below

The First View

The first view of Taksang Gompa, from the approach road towards the end of Paro valley can only be described as awesome. As I looked up towards the distant, peaks, half engulfed by mist rising from the valley below, the shrine buildings looked like two whitish dots almost like eyes carved on the vertical rocky cliff. As I focused, it looked more like the head of a giant "yeti" staring down towards the valley with menacing eyes. The top of the cliff with scattered tree line almost resembled the head of the "Yeti" of my wild imagination. The rising mist surrounding the cliff in patches added to the eerie atmosphere. It looked cold, distant and menacing. That was Taksang Gompa, perched on a cliff face, like two white specks stuck on the vertical rock by magical glue. I had first seen its photograph in a forwarded email in 2004, as one of the ten most precariously placed shrines in the world. It was so captivating that very moment I told myself that I would be there one day. That day was to be 16 Sep 2012.

Cliff Hanger

Pine Forest along the Mule Track

As we drove further up into the jungle along a mud track, the two dots cliff hanger appeared and disappeared from view through the tall pine trees. Finally we approached a clearing, a flat ground with more spaces between the interspersed pine trees. There were two SUVs parked and few Bhutanese men moving around. Two wooden huts built on a platform looked like make shift office. As the track ended here the place turned out to be the base for onward journey to the holy Gompa. I could see Taksang Gompa far up above looking more distant and dangerously vertical. The base, almost hidden within the pine trees served as a parking area for few vehicles, horses and mules. Morning sun filtered and sprayed through the thick canopy of pine trees touching the wet ground that was full of dry fallen leaves. The air was forest fresh and the gurgling sound of stream meandering down the mountain accentuated the freshness. The place was quiet except for the natural sound of scratch and scamper of squirrel or starling rush of a magpie that flew overhead in a hurry. I approached a Bhutanese man in his traditional attire "Gho" and asked him about the route to the Holy Shrine above. He indicated and explained that the trek route was the mule track spiraling up the mountain to Taksang Gompa. Seeing the parked SUVs I enquired if anyone had gone up that morning, I was pleasantly surprised to learn that no other than Her Highness; the young Queen of Bhutan herself had taken the route to Taksang Gompa early morning to offer prayers. Unlike the ever present red light gleaming, siren screaming cars, posse of gun wielding black cat commandos, hangers on and sycophants creating a big hullabaloo being the usual scene of a big or small time VIP visits in India, the place was quiet, peaceful and serene with no trace of the Queen having been there and would be there again upon her return.

A lesson, if it may be, for Indian VIPs on humility and simplicity by the young, beautiful, well-educated and well-bred silent queen. The queen's small entourages had quietly left on horseback for the holy shrine early morning. A small group of drivers and staff with 2 SUVs were waiting for her to return. I admire this young queen, recently married to the Oxford educated young king, His Highness, King Jigme Keshar Namgyal Wangchuk. A young and handsome couple made for each other and their small Himalayan Kingdom. God Bless them and their Shangri-La kingdom.

Handsome King of Bhutan, His Highness Jigme Khesar Namgyel Wangchuk & Beautiful Queen, Her Highness Jetsun Pema Wangchuk

(Pic from net-Courtesy Google)

"Great things are done when men and mountain meet."

-   *William Blake*

The Trek to Taksang

We set out for the trek, carrying back packs with water, biscuits and fruits. We crossed the stream, stepping on the stones placed for the purpose, and started climbing uphill. The track was initially gradual ascent over wet ground, spiraling up through the pine forest as it appeared and disappeared along the bushes and trees, playing hide and seek. A Bhutanese man sitting under a tree with couple of ponies grazing around yelled at us offering to rent his pony for the climb @ INR 1000.00. We politely refused and moved on. The path was indeed the mule track with few short cuts, spread like exposed roots of a giant tree, made by the locals. Such short cuts are usual all over the hills. We kept to the mule track and mostly avoided the steep short cuts.

A group of playful young boys and girls came rushing up and overtook us, laughing, giggling and shouting as they did. The track became steeper and our movement slower. We trudged on, one foot forward at a time. A pack of load carrier mules with their drivers crossed us on their way down; leaving fresh dung on the track that was immediately attacked by green flies. It looked natural and not at all dirty, a part of the jungle trail.

Crossing the Mule Pack

Some more local families overtook us and surged forward at a fast pace, almost a routine walk for them. I wanted to keep my own steady pace using the umbrella as walking stick. At the age of 68, one needs to listen to one's body and not rush to compete with others. We pushed every step, slow and steady and continued climbing. My thigh and calf muscles started aching demanding rest. As we kept climbing my breathing became harder and started roaring into my ears. We trudged on. The mountain breeze, when it came, helped me like a breath of fresh air. A crow hovered upwind in search of a prey perhaps. The climb became grimmer as we continued to angle towards the top. My shirt, which had been soaked with sweat, now felt stiff and uncomfortable. I wiped the perspiration from my forehead that was trickling into my eyes. I glanced at the rock face towards my right and saw the holy Gompa across that looked like toy houses stuck together on the rock face with glue. It became bigger as we climbed further up and reduced the distance with the rock face. We pushed slowly with no sense of hurry. The aroma of the jungle was printed on every whiff of breeze that I savored. The mist rose from the valley below and started blotting out the tumbled slopes of the rocky cliff below the Gompa.

After about an hour and a half we reached a midpoint, rested and sipped water. It would be unwise to rest for too long as once the body gets cold it will be difficult to climb up, better keep the body warm and maintain the rhythm of the climb.

Cheerful Friend along the way

We came across a young and smart Bhutanese man working for a tour company. We chatted and took photograph for remembrance, a smiling mountain man as ever. As we walked on and reached higher ground we could see the majestic Taksang Gompa through the trees, perched like a bird's nest on a vertical cliff. More we saw it from closer distance more precariously placed it looked.

Taksang Gompa shrouded by Mist

A view of Taksang Gompa from the Prayer Wheel Ground

Half way up the hill and about two hours climb we reached a plain area with rows of prayer wheels under a small tin roof. Pilgrims, both locals and tourists were resting on their way up and down. Young Bhutanese boys were playing innovative cricket with stone wicket and locally made bat and ball. The cricket fever has reached nooks and corners of the mountains without sparing any community and people. Across the plain area and prayer wheels was a rough wooden signboard written "Cafeteria" indicating the way across a gate. It felt good to see the sign board, tempting to change direction to relish a hot cup of tea, but we walked on towards our destination. The path flattened for some time and we could see some houses far above, a small village. We came across a clear water stream gurgling down across the path. We drank straight from it, sweet water of mountain spring untouched by pollution created by civilization. I pray such purity in small doses stay forever in these mountains.

Fresh Spring Water

"Tread softly for this is holy ground. It may be, could we look with seeing eyes, this spot we stand upon is paradise"

- *Christina Rossetti*

The Final Assault

At the end of the flat stretch of the track I saw a huge conical rock and a slab of huge flat stone. A young man was sitting on the slab, his back towards us. As I reached the Conical Stone, I realised it was the view point offering a crystal clear view of Taksang Gompa across the deep gorge that separated us and the vertical rock face holding Taksang Gompa. It was an awesome sight, The Holy Gompa in real just in front of me stuck on the rock face. It is known by the name "Copper-Colored Mountain Paradise of Padmasambhava". It was just like the numerous photos I had seen, a dream like experience that will be etched in my memory for ever. This is the view point for visitors below which there is a small cafeteria to provide refreshments. The trek beyond this point is very scenic with the sound of the water fall breaking the silence. Along the trek route prayer flags strewn across the gorge between the View Point Mountain and the Taksang Gompa side of the cliff add spiritual beauty to the place. I sat on the stone slab, touched the conical stone, imbibing the calm and serenity of the place, my tiredness and aching limbs vanished. Here the air was fresh and clear with all the crispness of high peaks and a sense of limitless distance. It had taken us 3 hours to get to this view point from the base.

The View Point

49

Steep Staircase to Waterfall   **The Tiger's Lair**

The last lap was the toughest; from the view point we had to go down about 500 feet along almost vertical cemented steps with hand railings, mercifully. Down below, at the end of the descent was Small Bridge over which cascaded a water fall from more than 1000 feet above. Against the grey verticality of the cliff, strand of milk like water continuously vanished into misty smoke atomized by the never ending crash on to the rock below and reappeared again in reconstituted form of liquid water that continued to flow down the gorge in an endless pursuit of nowhere. I could not take my eyes off this miracle of water. We are so fascinated by the flow of water that we stare fixedly at it for prolonged period of time, never getting tired of seeing, whether it is sea, river, waterfall, fountain, pond, lake or a small stream. Strange, as it may seem but we seem to be biased towards fascination with water against land. It is odd because the land is varied, colorful and endless as against the consistency of water. The bias may be so because water is in a state of constant movement while the land is static and the movement of land or the movement of leaves and branches of trees as also the movement of earth's crust is imperceptible to us. It is this visible movement of water particles whether in the form of concentric ripples on a lake or the rumbling fall on the rocks that defines the purity of water with vibrant impulse. That is why water is water, the essence of life.

We started the steep descent of steps slowly holding the hand rails thoughtfully built for the aged and tired pilgrims. We passed many visitors, Bhutanese, Indians, Japanese and other nationals. As we reached the foot bridge we were covered by never ending spray of misty foamy water from the water fall. It was a heavenly experience, tired as we were; the cooling effect was mentally and physically soothing. I could have stayed there forever.

The Waterfall

After crossing the footbridge passing through the gauntlet of misty spray we reached the ascending flight of equally steep steps rising up towards the Holy Shrine, the final climb for the final destination. After climbing the trail for three hours and reaching an altitude of 10000 plus feet I was so tired that I could only move forward one step at a time holding the hand rails. If I am tired I am tired, I am aware of the tiredness and revolting muscles of my body. Awareness is important, it is like going inside one's body and knowing, that takes the pain away. The fact that I ventured to undertake this trek was good enough for me,

to bite what I could chew, defining aim that can be achieved. To know how far one can stretch the body up to and little beyond the limit of endurance. To this thought I fit in my own philosophy of life, "Age is a matter of mind, if you don't mind, it does not matter", let age not

Steep Staircase Waterfall to Tiger's Lair

51

be a factor for what we wish to do and what we wish to achieve. It can be done.

Up Close the Tiger' Lair

Finally we reached the formidable shrine, the Holy Taksang Gompa and I had finally realised my dream. As we stepped on the first platform of the Gompa there was a small make shift check post, manned by few RBP (Royal Bhutan Police) personnel where we had to leave our back packs, cameras, cell phones etc. No such thing as coupon and pigeonhole system. There were nails on the walls of the check post where visitors hung their bags. Having finished with the formalities of giving our names that a police man wrote on the crumpled dog eared register, we climbed on to the second platform. It lead to a dark tunnel like pathway under a roof that opened to a small open courtyard. I was aware that I was standing on the small ledge of the great cliff that served as this courtyard. Anther five steps and I would be at the very edge of the almost bottomless vertical cliff. I took those five steps and looked down and saw the vertical rock face down below. I quickly retraced my steps back. At the end of the courtyard, at ground level, stuck to the rock face was a door that led to a small cave like shrine. As I entered the door, I noticed that the left wall of the shrine had a small, window like closed door. It was the door to the cave where Guru Rinpoche (Padmasambhava) had meditated in 8th century. The door was locked and I was told by a lama that it is opened only once a year. I touched my forehead on the ground next to the door and felt blessed.

Guru Padmasambhava- 8 Circa

Upon coming out of the small shrine we were guided upstairs across a flight of narrow wooden staircase. At the first floor as I was ushered into the holy shrine. There was the main alter over which were placed the idols of Gautam Buddha, Guru Rinpoche and Maa Tara. Below on the second shelf were rows of *Chimies* or glowing butter lamps, next row were water offerings in small silver bowls. There were offerings of flowers, eatables such as biscuits, sweets, fruits and homemade *Khapsey*, (deep fried and hard bread in many folds), all neatly arranged on plates and wooden baskets on the high alter. The fine scented aroma of *Sang*, (holy essence) made by burning dry pine leaves and herbs in a metal container with chains to hold and swing, added to the holy fervor of the shrine. It was so bright and lively as if the spirit Guru Rinpoche was present. An elderly lama was sitting on a low cushioned platform opposite the main alter reading "*holy Poshtak*" (quatrains) written in "Zongkhar", Bhutanese script, on rectangular papers, neatly arranged and bound by cloth and wooden slabs from the top and bottom. I sat next to the lama and asked for his blessings. Most kindly he blessed me by touching my head with his small prayer staff and gave me dark seeds that would have been blessed. I tried to prolong my stay inside the holy shrine as much as possible but I had to make room for other pilgrims. As we left the shrine we were given our share of Holy "Prasad" that included *Khapsey*, fruits and biscuits. Upon coming out we stepped down to the first platform there was a small pond of spring water that was materializing from under a huge rock. Like others I collected a bottle of this holy water and carried it along.

It was with a deep sense of satisfaction, gratitude and spiritual feeling that I started descending down the steps to the foot bridge and up towards the view point. Although tired and knees creaking, I took photographs of the shrine and waterfall. Finally after what seemed like forever, we reached the view point. The small tea stall was nonfunctional at this point of time but I entered a small chapel adjacent and lighted 7 *Chimies* @ INR 45 per lamp and continued my ascent to the view point. This time the aim was to reach the cafeteria next to the Prayer Wheel area to try our luck with some hot food. It started drizzling but the elation and satisfaction of having reached Taksang Gompa was too high to worry about the drizzle or for that matter even a heavy rain. I had lived my dream.

We reached the cafeteria that already had the Japanese group helping themselves over lunch buffet. The dining hall was a huge, almost 50 meters by 30 meters in size with a long table serving hot food and rows of Bhutanese style low divans with matching low tables called *Choksey* to keep plates and mugs. We paid INR 450 per plate and helped ourselves from the well laid buffet of vegetarian food. The bill of fare was steamed rice, lentil soup, different types of vegetables cooked in Bhutanese way in cottage cheese and Chilies. After the sumptuous lunch there was salty butter tea called "*shuza*" that we could have as many cups. We exited the cafeteria and I took more photographs of the holy shrine now surrounded by mist. After a quick visit to the loo we left the cafeteria and started back downhill. There was a huge Bhutanese mastiff sitting quietly under a tree near the Cafeteria not at all minding the drizzle or the people passing by. Its mood was sober to say the least, not at all hostile. I shot him with camera, said goodbye as he gave me an unconcerned look and we moved on. I seem to come across such dogs most of the places I visit, "Karmic" Connection.

Trek back was comparatively easy; however we had to be careful of the slippery track with the continuing drizzle. It was heartening to see the group

Karmic Friend

of young boys and girls running down the track, slipping, holding each other's hands, giggling and shrieking. All very happy. A lone and elderly western lady was being helped by a young Bhutanese couple as they took careful steps down the slippery path. The Japanese group was also walking down alongside us, all happy and satisfied. Although it had taken us 3 hours plus to reach Taksang Gompa from the base, it took us only about one and half hours to return. As we crossed the clear stream of the base most of us rubbed the mud from our shoes on the watery stones. Finally we climbed into our Scorpio and drove back to the resort, a half an hour drive. That night we celebrated with a fine Bhutanese rum and coke that we had bought in Paro general Store. Next day we returned along the long highway back to Siliguri with lunch break in Jaigaon. It was a trip to remember for all times to come for we had lived our dreams of visiting the world's one of the 10 most precariously placed shrines, Taksang Gompa.

The Legend of Taksang Gompa

This holy shrine, Taksang is Spelt and pronounced in Tibetan as "Stag Tshang" meaning "Tiger's lair". As per the legend in 8th Century Guru Padmasambhava (Guru Rinpoche) flew to this location from Tibet on the back of his tigress consort so as to tame the Tiger demon. He meditated in the same cave for 3 months, 3 weeks, 3 days and 3 hours. Another legend says that a former wife of an emperor of Tibet Yeshe Tsogyal, willingly became a disciple of Guru Rinpoche, transformed herself into a tigress and carried the Guru on her back from Tibet landing on the cliff, which he "anointed" as the place for

55

building a monastery. He established Buddhism and the Nyingmapa school of Mahayana Buddhism in Bhutan, and has been considered the "protector saint of Bhutan. After his meditation the Guru Rinpoche emerged in eight incarnated forms. Thereafter the place became holy and came to be known as the "Tiger's Nest". It is further believed that Taksang Monastery was built by King Tenzin Rabgye in 1692. It has been mentioned by authors that it was Guru Padmasambhava who had reincarnated again in the form of Tenzin Rabgye.

The Monastery, Fire and Rebuilding

The monastery is located 15 kms North of Paro and hangs on a precipitous cliff at 3,120 M (10,240 ft.), about 900 M (3,000 ft.) above the Paro valley, on the right side of the Paro Chu (water). Though it looks formidable, the monastery complex has access from several directions; the North West path through the forest, from the South along the mule track generally used by visitors and tourists, and from the North, access over the rocky plateau, which is called the "Hundred Thousand Fairies" known as Bumda.

On 19th April 1998, a fire broke out in the main building of the monastery complex, which contained valuable paintings, artifacts and statues. The fire is believed to have been caused by electrical short-circuit or a flickering butter lamps lighting the hanging tapestries. A monk also died during the fire. The restoration works were undertaken at an estimated cost of 135 million ngultrum (Bhutanese Currency). The Government of Bhutan and the then King of Bhutan, Jigme Singhye Wangchuk, oversaw the restoration of the damaged monastery and its contents in 2005.

"Nothing is more expensive than a start"

- Friedrich Nietzsche

The Beginning of Journey

It was a spur of the moment decision to take this trip to Bhutan without much plans, aim, mission and vision. Such unplanned trips, more often than not, turn out to be the best and most memorable ones. When a dear friend decided to come all the way from Afghanistan to pay me a visit I decided on this trip. However, at the back of mind there was Taksang Gompa, one of the ten most precariously placed shrines in the world that I had to see for myself. When we took off from Siliguri on 13th Sep 2012 in my Scorpio, the idea was to drive straight to the capital Thimpu and that is what we did albeit after a night halt in Phuntsoling, the Bhutanese border town adjacent to India's last frontier town, Jaigaon. Distance between Siliguri and Phuntsoling is 94 kms.

The drive along the National Highway 31 from Siliguri to Sevoke (21 Kms.), especially after Salugara, a small Bhutia and Gorkha dominated bazaar on the outskirts of Siliguri, was smooth over well carpeted road. Incidentally, this small bazaar Salugara is quite on the international map because of presence of "Kalachakra", a holy Buddhist monastery where His Holiness the Dalai Lama comes periodically to perform the "Wong (World Peace) Prayers" that is attended by thousands of devotees from the Darjeeling hills, Sikkim, Bhutan and Nepal. I have noticed that one prominent personality who also visits the place is no other than Hollywood Actor, Richard Gere. Almost adjoining Salugara is the Sevoke Military Cantonment with neat and well laid out barracks, gardens and freshly mowed lush green lawns. Most of the Military cantonments all over the world are alike with neat clean areas, well laid out blooming gardens, rows of neat barracks and lawns to match. It is heartening that Indian Army is now on a warpath towards environmental up gradation promoting greenery and eco preservation in all cantonments. Nature caring Army is good for the health of the country. After crossing the cantonment on either side of the National Highway the smooth, well carpeted road knifes through a packed jungle on either side right up to Sevoke. Thereafter it is another 3 kms of zigzag road up to the historic Coronation or Tiger Bridge that spans across Teesta River rumbling down to the plains from North Sikkim.

NH-31 across Sevoke Forest

Coronation Bridge was named to commemorate the coronation of King George VI. The design and planning of the bridge was carried out by John Chambers, the last British Executive Engineer of Darjeeling PWD. The construction by Gammon India, Bombay commenced in 1937 and completed in 1941. Unimaginable today but the cost of construction then was INR 4 lakhs. RCC Bridge is supported by a fixed arch, which has its two ends fixed on rock layers on either side of the river. Way back in early 50s, travelling with my father from Kalimpong to Siliguri I used to look at this bridge in complete awe. 72 years old and going strong but there is definitely a need to preserve this historic bridge by proper maintenance and traffic regulation, specially keeping in view that the engineering design of the bridge built then may not have catered for the continuous rumbling heavy traffic of today carrying thousands of tons of loads every day to and from Bhutan and the seven North Eastern States. Hope the Government is listening.

After the Bridge, condition of the road is not so good and pot holes start appearing and disappearing. We cross Mongpu, a small bazaar with a forest check post about 5 kms from Coronation Bridge, and pass through "Dooars" area. As the name suggests, it means a gateway to Bhutan from North Bengal plains. The Dooars valley is paradise of biodiversity with combination of thick forest that stretches up to Nepal and Bhutan, famous wild life sanctuaries and numerous Tea Gardens in its lap. In other words it is greenery all along except for the villages and bazaars dotting the National Highway. It has Jaldapara

Coronation Bridge over Teesta River, Sevoke

Wild Life Sanctuary, Buxa National Park, Chapramari Wild Life Reserve and Mahanada Wild Life Sanctuary. Gaps between forest areas and wild life sanctuaries are covered by acres and acres of green carpeted tea gardens on either side of the road, another British legacy. Teesta River and its numerous tributaries spiral down from Sikkim to Sevoke through Dooars.

For lunch we had tea, hot *Samosas* and *Jalebi* in a roadside sweet shop in Maal Bazar, half way to Jaigaon. In my opinion, while travelling, even in a not so hygienic road side dhaba or sweetshop, any food that is sizzling hot from the pot is safer to eat and that's the norm I follow while travelling. As we drove along, the last about 10 kms to Jaigaon was a driver's nightmare. The National Highway degenerated in to a dusty crater filled apology for a road. The whole highway was replaced by ugly craters and unending cloud of dust. Heavily loaded rumbling trucks from the North East States and Bhutan were precariously balancing between deep craters. Some trucks had fallen by the way side unable to manage their center of gravity in deep craters. Unfortunately, India's National Highway to Bhutan and the only land link to the Seven Sisters of the North East States had degenerated into a national shame. I understand it is improved now. But how a Government can allow a National Highway of such strategic importance to come to such a mess is beyond one's imagination. I can only say, "It happens only in India".

Another Country-Land of the Thunder Dragon

Finally after what seemed an endless crater driving, we reached Jaigaon, another small township slightly bigger than a bazaar. As we crossed the gate and entered Phuntsoling, it was a different world. It was a refreshing change from the chaos of normal Indian Bazaar of horn blaring traffic, senseless parking, crisscrossing cyclists and cycle rickshaws to quiet and orderly kingdom. Bhutanese style rows of buildings lining the main road that was well regulated with disciplined traffic and parking. We checked into Hotel Dragon Inn, a medium range Hotel with complete Bhutanese décor, neat and tidy. By the time it had started drizzling and we decided to stay indoors and check the bar and restaurant. The hotel including the restaurant was staffed by young Bhutanese girls in "Kira", their traditional wrap around skirt like dress with loose brocade coat with big and folded sleeves. Little girls looked very smart and sober. We had vegetarian dinner in the restaurant and retired to our rooms so as to get early morning start the next day for long drive to Thimpu.

A Bhutanese Family in Traditional Dress

(Pic from net-Courtesy Google)

Next morning, obtaining the permit to enter Bhutan, even with the help of our Travel Agent representative, took us about 3 hours, shuttling as we did, between the two sides of bureaucracy, Indian Consulate and Bhutanese counterpart as also the Bhutanese RTO Office for the Vehicle Permit. We could finally start only around 11 am. Distance from Phuntsoling to Thimpu is 180 kms and the road climbs up through steep gradient to Richending, 1312 feet, and a distance of 5 kms from Phuntsoling. It has a Check Post where permit to enter Bhutan papers are checked and stamped by the Police. There is also a famous Kharbandi Gompa on the ridge line offering a good view of Dooars plain. After clearing the papers we drove on along the highway which takes a long twisting and turning climb through tropical jungle with few hamlets along the way. From Gedu the road somewhat levels as it runs along the ridge line offering spectacular view of landscape, meandering river and waterfalls. Thereafter it is a combination of up and downhill drive up to Chapchala ridge from where the road descends down to gorge and follows the river upstream to the river confluence and road junction at Chunzom where we find another check point. From here a road branches off to left leading to Paro and Haa and the main road continues alongside the river to Thimpu.

The traffic was thin and not at all crowded with only few SUVs, cars and Indian trucks plying up down the road. There was no restaurant or *dhaba* enroute, we missed the ever present road side *dhabas* that dot the Indian Highways. A small wayside village called Kamji with few houses, half way across; served us much needed hot cup of tea. We opted against ever present Maggie noodles and settled for some biscuits and fried *pakoras* that we struggled to chew. We also bought cottage cheese and cucumber to munch on the way. As we slowly cruised along the highway and entered the capital I could feel the distinct difference the disciplined Bhutanese traffic as against the chaotic Siliguri traffic where cycle rickshaws and Auto rickshaws, load carrier cycle rickshaws called *Thela* are the kings of the roads. Thimpu was a disciplined traffic, no traffic police and no horns that I felt rather odd and unnatural having experienced the Indian roads all my life.

We hit Thimpu proper at about 5.30 pm and found our hotel, Dragon Route, bang on the main street near the public square. It was drizzling but the weather was cool and pleasant. Wearing hat and a light jacket helped. We checked in and found the rooms with country type pine wood paneled walls and wooden floors. It was getting dark so without wasting time, just after a cup of tea, we set off to experiment the capital street with a look-see walk.

The street was clean and lined by weeping willow trees that looked very nice. The buildings were Bhutanese style architecture that had four to five storeys. We walked through light drizzle along the stone paved sidewalk. Surprisingly a melodious and rhythmic Western music filled the air; the source of the melody was a small open air stand that was extension of the main street. It looked quite unusual to see Bhutanese boys in traditional dress playing and crooning Western Tuned Bhutanese songs. A group of about 100 young men and women, gathered around the band stand were gyrating with the melody and rhythm of the music. All were wearing Bhutanese traditional dress, no jeans, pants and skirts. The dress code is strict; men wear "*Gho*" a kimono like knee length gown type of dress, tied by a long kamarbandh with long shocks and shoes. Women's dress is called, "*Kira*", an elegant wrapped around skirt like with a check or brocade jacket for the top. Both Tibetan and Bhutanese dress is alike except for few variations. There is also the marked difference in the material used in Bhutan. Whereas Tibetan men and women fancy any type of clothing materials for their "*Bakkhu*", Bhutanese use only the traditional and colorful Bhutan made check cloth material for their "*Gho*" and "*Kira*".

Side Walk in Thimpu, Men & Women in "Gho" & "Kira"
(Pic from net-Courtesy Google)

Modern Bhutan, with two party democracy, has come long way from the old feudal Bhutan. As per a UN census Bhutan has the highest level of

"Gross Happiness" compared to all the countries of the world. It is truly said that quantum of happiness is the result of number of desires fulfilled. More the desire lesser the fulfillment, resultantly lesser happiness. TV was allowed only few years back and the Western Culture in terms of dress is not allowed. I guess this is the only way to preserve the heritage and culture of this Small mountain nation. If the flood gate of Western Culture is opened it will take no time to engulf this Kingdom and its simple people. The name of the band was aptly "Ozone Layer". Modernized but well-grounded at the base of their culture, tradition and discipline.

Feeling hungry but not wanting to eat dinner yet, we walked into to, what looked like a beautiful & homely cottage restaurant at the corner of the main street. It looked cozy and homely but alas the look did not match the bakery product. We had tea and some pastry look alike on self-service and left in a hurry. The tempo of drizzle seemed to accelerate towards full blast rain, and it was time for dinner, so we walked into a cane and bamboo interiors restaurant on the main street. I was looking forward to sample few drinks of the new country but there was nothing much displayed in the bar. Except for the national product whisky there was no rum or brandy or other "foreign liquor" that we are so used to. I asked the barman if they had tinned Tibetan "*Chhang*", rice beer, made in Tibet that I had sampled in Sikkim having changed hands in Nathula Border Trade. I was told it was illegal to have that kind of import. We decided to give the usual drinks a miss and ordered dinner of Momo, Thukpa (Noodle soup) and salad, nothing much to talk home. We walked back to the hotel and slept early.

The next morning, Thimpu was still awash with continuous drizzle. The days plan was to visit Paro and return. Then I wondered aloud "return and do what" as there was nothing much to explore in Thimpu except for rows and rows malls filled with consumer items from Thailand, China and Malaysia. Friend came with the idea as to why not shift to Paro, explore the old town. We checked out and headed for Paro and rang up travel agent to fix us a hotel there. Good feeling to be on the road again, a purpose to go to a new place, excitement especially so when we came to know that Paro is a very picturesque place with nature's bounty a plenty.

Countryside Road to Paro

We drove back on the same road towards Phuntsoling. Just outside Thimpu there were apple orchards almost bordering the road and roadside stalls selling fresh apples from the orchard. We could see apple trees bowing down with weight of too many apples. It was a luxurious availability of just plucked fresh apples and it was only prudent to buy some to relish the freshness. We bought some and ate along the way, juicy and fresh. After about 25 kms drive we reached Chunzom and got our papers checked before taking the right turn to Paro. The traffic to Paro was light with very few vehicles on the road. We passed through another cluster of roadside shops selling apples and vegetables, I snapped three little girls, in their *Kira* going to school, giggling. Children all over the world are the same, apotheosis of innocence, no care in the world, no tension and not at all affected by the environment. We drove on savoring the green freshness of the country side, valleys of yellowish rice fields dotted with trees and hemmed in by hills that stretched beyond the horizon.

The road to Paro was silky smooth appearing and disappearing along the many folds of the mountain of Alpine forests. We passed through many "*Chortens*" along the highway. "*Chorten*" meaning a "container", a space for worship or offerings, also built in memories of Lamas, High Officials or to protect a place a path or an area such as cross roads, high mountain passes against evil spirits. Perhaps the culture of these Chortens date back to old Bon Religion as it is believed to be in existence even before the emergence of Buddhism in to the land. The architecture of these Chortens are based on

Girls to School

5 elements; the square base symbolizes the earth, the half dome symbolizes water, the conical spire symbolizes fire, the crescent moon and the sun atop symbolizes air and vertical spike symbolizes the light and wisdom of the Buddha. Such Chortens are seen abundantly in Ladakh.

Chorten

First landmark we came across on way to Paro was the one and only Airport of Bhutan, a beautiful land strip located in the Valley, surrounded by green fields and misty mountains on either side. Few kilometers before entering Paro Town, almost hugging the Paro Chu (river), we were greeted by the majestic presence of Paro Dzong (Fort), an imposing citadel built in Circa 1646 that now houses government offices. A wooden bridge, perhaps as old as the dzong, leading to the main entrance that is guarded by two deities on either side; a Mongolian man holding a Tiger on a leash and another man holding a black yak, as the guarding deities. The building has a very beautiful and unique old Bhutanese style wood work that would have been carved by experts in the trade of yore that date back to almost 500 years ago. Just above the Paro Dzong stands another edifice called "Ta-Dzong" meaning watch tower that now houses the museum.

Paro Dzong (Fort)

After crossing the Paro Dzong as we entered Paro town, I was awestruck by this out of the world scenario. It was like we were lifted from the modern world of concrete jungle and chaotic traffic to the most serene, peaceful Shangri-La in a different world, except, perhaps for the presence of few modern transport plying or parked along the roadside; Paro was original, pure and traditional Bhutan. Both sides of the main road were lined by traditional stone-wood Bhutanese style buildings that housed shops, restaurants etc. A building with grocery shop had the King's photo prominently displayed.

66

Paro Street

A Shop Building with King's Photo

We met our guide who took us to our destination, Galling Resort, about 3 kms away from town along a graveled road. Located on the banks of Paro chu; the property was tastefully constructed and painted in unique mud color ethnic Bhutanese style. The view from the balcony was breathtaking with Paro Chu rumbling right in front across the road, part of Paro beyond and finally the valley rising to meet the misty mountains that made the distant horizon. Anyone with an eye for the nature or a plain nature lover is bound to be enchanted by the natural beauty, landscape that would make not spending couple of days almost impossible. We did just that. The resort was warm, comfortable with a cozy lounge, wood paneled bedroom and comfortable attached bath. Our rooms had the same view as balcony and decided to keep the curtains drawn and windows opened so as to be part of the beautiful view.

A view from Khaling Resort, Taksang Gompa is on the Misty Mountain Ahead

After a hot cup of welcome tea and biscuits we saw our rooms rather suits and drove back to town for a look see and browse the shops. For lunch we walked in to a restaurant and ordered Vegetable momo, soup and *ema thachi*, Bhutanese dish of cottage cheese and chili. We enquired after the general direction, route and location of Taksang Gompa and drove towards that direction. We drove through a beautiful country side and passed through golden paddy fields. We crossed ruins of an old Dzong (fort) spread across large area. After about 10 kms the road started climbing up gradually making twists and turns as it did. There were small cottage lodges and a cafeteria as also couple of houses, Chorten before the road entered pine forest. After driving for about 5 kms of gradual uphill track we came to a clearing as the road came to an end. We looked around the area for a while and concluded that this place would be the base for onward journey to Taksang Gompa. It was confirmed by a villager collecting pine cones for his hearth. We returned back to the resort. I decided to trek the next day morning. At night, we had our usual drinks in the room and dinner at the main dining room. It was a peaceful sleep soothed by the steady sound of river, Paro-chu, flowing across the property. Next day we would trek to Taksang Gompa.

"The great end of life is not knowledge but action"

- TH Huxley

Namprikdang Of Dzongu
The Lepcha Country Of North Sikkim

"Wandering re-establishes the original harmony which once existed between man and nature"

– Anatole France

What "Shangri-La" is to the world, "Mayal Lyang" is to Lepcha Tribe, It is believed that good Lepchas, when they pass from this life, go and live in Mayal Lyang for ever. It seems to be heaven indeed.

Namprikdang, as we see it today, is a small flat land on the banks of Teesta River, cocooned in the pristine nature's lap within the Kanchenchunga biosphere in Dzongu area of North Sikkim, India. The ancestors of the Lepcha tribe of Dzongu are believed to be the aboriginals of the mythical Mayal Lyang. As many other lands lost to the civilization, this land was also as pure as they come, untouched and uncorrupted by the civilization. Late Arthur Foning, a true Lepcha, has described the natural purity of North Sikkim in forties and fifties in his book, "Lepchas, my Vanishing Tribe".

A Water fall in Dzongu

Around the first half of the nineteenth century, British overlords, after establishing suzerainty over Sikkim, had initiated the process of establishing "Lepcha Reserve" in Dzongu; however, finally, it was only in early sixties that the late Chhogyal of Sikkim declared the area reserve for the Lepcha Community.

A Lepcha Couple of Yore

Ancient Travelers of Dzongu

In the prehistory of time, in the legendary and mythical Mayal Lang country, at the foothills of the mighty Kanchendzonga and in the lap of Dzongu valley, there was a small and beautiful cradle of the nature called Namprikdang. It is believed to have been formed by fast flowing glacier fed river, Teesta. Today, Namprikdang sits at the confluence of Rangyu (Teesta River) and the hills of Dzongu. As we see it today, Namprikdang is a tiny grassy flatland oasis by the bank of the Teesta River covered by thick forest with perpetual green of willow groves. Long distance travellers of ancient times long gone by, walking long days along these jungle tracks, hiding and appearing behind the concavity of the mountains, could have found this beautiful flatland by the bank of the river as a natural resting place for the night. Those travellers would have struck camps in the last of the day light and moved about looking for firewood to make campfire. During such times, the air would have been frigid with cold and the travellers would have seen the puff of their breath in the red and purple after glow of the sun. At this very place, ancestors of today's Lepchas would have made fire in their primitive ways with stones and flints, throwing slices of dried meat into the fire along with herbs, edible roots and plants for dinner. They would have relished the natural roasts with "*satto*" or "*Champa*" (powdered gram/ barley/rice as "ready to eat meals") and perhaps washed it down with home brewed "*chhang*" (country wine) from their bamboo flasks. Sitting across the campfire and talking in low whispers, those travellers of the past would have exchanged their ancient thoughts across the camp fire flames dancing between them. Finally, tired and weary by long day's march, they would have laid over their yak skin mattress upon soft grassy ground, putting a hand between the cheek and the stone pillow below and drifted off to sleep, albeit into their ancient dreamland. After the sound of the breathing became long and steady, a fellow companion, a wife, brother, sister or a friend would have looked at the sleeping companion with an expression that would be like love. Their concept of time would have been the movement of the sun or moon or shadows of the virgin mountains falling over the green pristine valleys.

Namprikdang today, the bridge across forever Mythical Mayal Country

Today's chronometers of time flashing hours, minutes and seconds would have been meaningless to those ancient men and women. In a sense, they lived outside the timeframe of modern world that seems to imprison human beings of today. Come dawn, as the stars began to pale off while the morning breeze blew over the ambers of the camp fire, the ancient ones would awake, freshen themselves by the river, shoulder their humble possessions, offer prayers and trudge along towards another sunset, across another mountain. Not very hard to imagine the world of difference between the foot travellers of the past with today's metro sexual people driving Boleros, Scorpios and Sumos on the same mountains albeit along carpeted tarmac roads instead of through bridges across the same Teesta River and mountains passes blasted off, echoing and shaking the countryside, making way for the civilization to invade and occupy the secret privacy of mother nature. These fast forward modern travellers of today would aim to reach Gangtok, Singtam Rangpo or Siliguri in two to four hours flat and walk into their cosy homes or hotel bars to down Black Labels, Foster's or Breezers with uncle chips and kababs or junk food.

The world has indeed changed and moved on. Organic and healthy life of the past, dubbed uncivilized and undeveloped by the modern people, has, almost pathetically, given way to synthetic metro life of today with all the creature comforts to boot, at a great cost. Defying the unavoidable changes and trapped in the civilized world, Namprikdang lives on.

The Legends of Namprickdang

"*Namprik*" in Lepcha language is the name of a bird and "*Kyong*" means stream, whereas "*Dang*" means flat land. The legend has it that a Namprik, the bird, used to visit this stream to drink the clean and pure holy water, hence the name, *Namprikdang*. Another legend says that there was a fight between two mountains, *Rongdokchu* and *Songfoklyo* and when *mount Kanchendzonga* learnt about it, he sent *Manik-Chu, the river* to bring about peace. This peace treaty was settled at *Namprikdang*. Yet another legend says that *Jamphimongs (Yetis)* used to comedown to this place from the high Himalayas every year for their yearly ablution. Another story goes that in times long gone by, Lepchas from nearby by villages used to seek blessings of the river at *Namprikdang* before proceeding on a voyage and offer thanks giving prayers upon safe return.

This version of the legend seems to be connected perhaps with historic facts. It makes sense to visualise that this beautiful place could have been the natural resting place for the travellers of the past and a place for offering prayers for safe journey, a ritual followed in many places around the world even today. Namprikdang is indeed a kind of nature's cradle right under the protective deity of the holy Mount Kanchendzonga and blessed on all sides by scenic mountains and hills of Dzongu.

Perhaps acknowledging the magnitude of rich significance and heritage of Namprikdang, to the Lepchas of past, present and future, the wise men and women of the tribe took the initiative to accord this holy place the importance it deserves in the annals of time. Accordingly, based on the legend, decided to mark the place as an everlasting monument of the Lepcha Tribe. This is how the most important annual function of the tribe, the Namsoong Festival, the Lepcha New Year, came to be celebrated at Namprikdang.

Legend of Namsoong

In the beginning of time, after creating the world with plants and animals, mother creator created a male and a female child each, brother and sister and called them *Fo-Dongthing* and *Nuzongnue* respectively. They were sent to the mystic land, Mayal Lyang by different routes with strict instructions not to meet on the way. However, on the way, while resting on either side of *Kohol Lake* they happened to see each other, attracted and cohabited. The result was the birth of a son. Fearing the wrath of their creator they hid the baby in a cave and went away. The child survived and grew up sucking its own limbs. In the mean time, due to the sin of incest *Fo-Dingthing and Nuzongnue* could not reach Mayal Lyang. Finally they were forgiven by the creator and blessed to live as husband and wife and procreate many children filling the country with human race. As the time passed by, there came sufferings, disaster and pain to the inhabitants. When wise men started exploring the cause of such sufferings it was revealed that sufferings was the creation of the first illicit son who had cursed his future brothers and sisters for the ill treatment meted out to him by his parents. People decided to face the evil and fight it out and started learning the art of war making weapons like bows, arrows, spears as also men with high spiritual powers called, as *Mun and Bunthung* were created to help mankind fight the evil. In the mean time the evil became more powerful and started changing its appearances, size and shape in the form of various animals from a rat to a pig.

The forms were rat, ox, tiger, eagle, dragon, snake, horse, ship, monkey, fowl, dog and pig. Finally the evil was destroyed in the form of a pig on the last day of the twelfth month of the Lepcha calendar, *Marlavo Tyangrigong.* The evil, due to its ability to change form just like the perfect organism in the concept of "Alien" was named *Lasso Mung* and his defeat is celebrated as victory of good over evil as *"Marlavo Tyangrigong Sonap"* every year. in short that is Lepcha New Year that is *Namsong Nambung.* It is this*Namsoong* festival that is celebrated every year at the Holy place, Namprikdang. To further commemorate the killing of the evil in the form of pig, a custom still exists to this day to slaughter a huge pig and offer it to the Chief Guest of the celebration. Needless to say that the Chief Guest is expected to reward the event by offering adequate incentives in the form of handsome amount of cash and favours. A good bargain or almost a great barter.

Back to the Present Reality

It is in this yearly Namsoong Festival of 2008-09 at Namprikdang, Dzongu held from 20 Dec 2008 to 4 Jan 2009 that I had the rare honour to be invited to play a humble part in this great and ancient event. As NGO committed to Relief and Rehalbitation programme in North Sikkim, I was invited with a request to organise a Free Health Camp on 3 & 4 Jan 2009 at Namprikdang during the Namsoong Festival. It was a rare opportunity to be a part of such legendary and ancient ritual even today. So our Medical Team proceeded from Mangan to the famous Namprikdang, half an hour drive down the valley on to the bank of River Teesta and established a Free Medical Camp for the benefit of villagers coming to celebrate Namsoong Festival. It was a rare honour to tread the same resting place of ancestors of Lepchas, people who rested at this very place by the same river or ancestors of the same trees that we can touch today. As we drive down a narrow but well paved road, we find ourselves on a flat land by the bank of Teesta; lo and behold this is Namprikdang, the old resting place of the ancestors Lepchas of Dzongu.

Misty Teesta

As we drive along, we are engulfed by thick foliage of well maintained forest nursery of few acres, thereafter there is a flat empty land that serves as football field as well as huge flat area used for fair. As we move along we are greeted by the beautiful traditional Lepcha House on a platform. It is built with modern cement and brick but made to look like the original version of wooden and bamboo structure. Finally, as if to commemorate the resting place of the ancestors there is a beautiful Forest Bungalow of the Government at the end of the flat land beyond which is Teesta River almost touching the foundation of the forest Guest House. Inside the traditional Lepcha House there are ancient pots, pans, weapons, utensils and photographs of ancient Lepcha couple. There. The hustle and bustle of generation of today has replaced the presence of a lonely traveller or a group of people resting at the same place but of very ancient times that can never be fathomed by the generation of today.

A Lepcha House

During this festival there are young and old, Lepchas and non Lepchas from nearby and far off villages. The people are happy, colourful and most of them donning traditional Lepcha dress. Ministers, Member of Legislative Assembly (MLAs), Village Panchayats, Government Officials sit on their majestic sofas at the VIP stand in the central VIP Stand with magnificent view of the entire festival. In the make shift restaurants people sit over hand woven yak wool rugs placed on mud floor smeared with cow dung. At the centre of the room is the ancient fire place of wrought iron tripod stand to keep pots and pan over fire called "*Odhan*". The menu hung on the wall along with display of ancient utensils is mouth watering meals fire roasted pork, beef, rice with *Chhang*, the local brew to wash the delicacies down. Having grown up amongst the same type of houses and among Lepcha neighbours and friends in Kalimpong, it was indeed heartening to connect with the ancient times at Namprikdang. Of course there was the official reception of VIPs in the traditional ways, the forgettable speeches after speeches, with clear and present hints to "vote for me". In spite of all these, the muck, the lack of toilet facilities, clean drinking facilities, high prices of food, people were enjoying themselves. I am sure the spirit of Mayal Country, its Legends would be smiling and blessing from up there, knowing the Great and holy Mount Kanchendzonga would be protecting Dzongu and Namprikdang forever, till the very end of times.

God Bless Namprikdang and keep it fresh and green forever with ever flowing Teesta River and fresh winds from Kanchendzonga.

This article is dedicated to Dimkit Lana Foning, an angel in Mayal Lyang now, Keep smiling your sweet smile dear Lana; guide and guard us forever.

■ ■

Life In Kabul- A Reflection

"All journeys have secret destinations of which the traveler is unaware."

Prelude

Ravaged over long years by series of coups, wars, Russian occupation and Taliban rule of terror, Afghanistan in circa 2006 was still a dangerous country to be in. In spite of defeat and dislodging of Taliban by US led NATO forces after of 9/11, followed by establishment of democratic government and the process of reconstruction under the aegis of UN underway, the country was still being riddled with continued Taliban terror attacks. Ambushes, rocket attacks, sniper killings, terror strikes anywhere, any time was business as usual in Afghanistan and the historic Kabul, being the epicenter, was bearing the brunt of it all. All this right under the nose of NATO forces, Afghan Army and Afghan Police. Many of these attacks were targeted at these very forces. In Kabul major landmarks such as Luxury hotels and embassies were the targets. In provinces kill list were the police, school and government officials. Abductions and ransom were snowballing into a fund raising industry.

THE SEATTLE TIMES

The Big Question

"Why would a 60 years old veteran, after 37 years of hard boiled Army life that included two bloody wars followed by 5 years in the banking service, in his right frame of mind, wish to work and live in Kabul, one of the most dangerous places on planet earth?" where as the alternative was to lead a quite retired life with golfing, reading and writing laced with evening pegs. The answer came easy, "It was the challenge, the risk, the adventure and bugging curiosity of the unknown. Frankly, greenback was only a part of the incentive not the whole. Another factor that contributed to my Kabul adventure was that my father, Pratap Singh Gahatraj had joined a mule and horse caravan along the old Silk Route, Kalimpong-Jelepla-Lhasa in mid 1920s and had lived and practiced dentistry there for 4 years. His tales about Tibet and the people, their culture and way of life used to be so fascinating that I wanted to hear more and more of his adventures. He used to speak fluent Tibetan and told us tales about their law system; how thieves and robbers used to be punished by dismembering hands and for antiseptic treatment the chopped wound used to be dipped in boiling oil. He talked about small pox outbreak in Tibet and how patients used to be treated by smearing pig fat all over their bodies and of the dead bodies that used to be chopped into pieces and fed to the vultures as a way of final offering to the nature and that they had separate caste to practice such rituals. I remember with quite disgust his narration about   the toilet system in old Tibet, the practice of passing stool through a hole in the designated room in the first floor and having the entire house hold excreta collected in another room in ground floor for the whole year to be used in the fields as manure. It was on hearing such strange and fascinating tales of another country that a seed of desire for travelling and experiencing other countries got embedded in my system. It is still in my bucket list to go to Lhasa by the famous Silk route; Kalimpong-Jelepla that my father followed around 100 years ago. Needless to say that Lhasa of my father's time has gone into oblivion but even today it is the same Lhasa, same soil, same mountains around and same Potala Palace. Such are the reasons that, as a humble tribute to my father's adventures in Tibet, I wanted to go to Afghanistan. Besides, I loved the idea of flying over Pakistan, across the Hindukush Mountains to experience the historic land that was traversed by legendary personalities like Tamburlaine and Babur with their marauding armies. I grabbed the offer and headed for Kabul.

All Good Things End but other Windows open

Like all good things in life, my pleasant five years in the Banking Service in Bhubaneswar, the capital city of Odisha state of costal India, was coming to an end as 2005 started closing. It was a happy and peaceful tenure in State Bank of India after a life time in Army uniform. The job was to oversee the security of 400 plus bank branches spread across the state. It involved extensive travelling, visiting branches across the state thereby experiencing the nooks, corners and people of the state. While not travelling, I played morning golf, attended 9 to 5 office and during evenings explored the city with my wife, watching movies, sampling gourmet restaurants and visiting parks. This is also the time I restarted golfing and became a regular at the Konark golf Course of the Army. During Sundays mornings, I played 18 holes golf in leisure with friends and on the way back home picked up varieties of sea food that my wife took pleasure to cook for a lazy Sunday lunch washing it down with chilled beer. It was the most peaceful, enjoyable and stable period of my life with zero tension, a sea changes from the hectic and nomadic Army Life. Five years, 2000 to 2005, in Odisha flew away like a sweet dream without a blink and suddenly I was going to be unemployed. The concept of old age and retirement had not entered my head, as such; I was ready for another job. No way could I visualise myself sitting at home and reading newspaper like a good retiree. In response to my Curriculum Vitae floating in the internet, I received a mail from a Beverage company in Dubai stating that they would be interested to have me in their team in Kabul as Chief Security Advisor. That was Dec 2005 and Afghanistan had been released from the yoke of violent tyrants and misogynist Taliban rule in 2001. I said yes and the phone interview that followed turned out to be a delightful conversation with the General Manager of the company, a Greek guy called Mike. After a pleasant talk of an interview when I asked him as to when I was required to join, he said, "yesterday".

Crossing Pakistan & the Hindukush

On 13 Dec 2005, just one month before my 60th birthday I was aboard an Air India flight bound for Kabul. As the pilot announced the entering of Pakistani air space I felt good to be crossing the neighbour, as ironically, I had faced the brunt of both the wars with them; 1965 in which, as a young soldier I nearly got killed in an ambush in Rajasthan sector and in 1971 as a young lieutenant I was wounded in action in J& K sector and I still carry the battle scar on my neck. That is another story. The mysterious land loomed under me in its surreal vastness of rugged mountains. This land had been witness to many battles and bloodsheds from eons of time that continues to this day. I imagined how fierce battles had been fought over the centuries, how many people had died how many had conquered only to meet death in another battle. Time rolled in this inhospitable brown rocky land but battles raged on from generation to generations, over the centuries. However, the fundamental theme of violence remained unchanged, that is to grab what belongs to others, become rich, famous and powerful. In a deep sense it is beyond logical comprehension as to why a set of humans wish to be powerful enough to enforce their way of life, culture and religion on the vanquished human beings. Why human beings always think their way of life is the best and every other should follow it. This is against the fundamentals of basic human right and dignity of every human being to follow a way of life, a culture and religion of choosing. If people understood this simple theme of creation there would be no wars, no boundaries. World would be one, just like the way John Lennon sang, "Imagine".

"Imagine there's no countries
It isn't hard to do
Nothing to kill or die for
And no religion too
Imagine all the people living life in peace"

Aerial View of the Hindukush

Life Begins in Kabul

After a smooth touchdown at Kabul International Airport under an overcast grey sky, as I stepped out of the plane and touched Afghanistan soil, I was greeted by a sunless, freezing December morning punctuated by gusts of chilling wind that touched my bones almost painfully. It was a major

81

environmental change, from the scorching heat of central India to the Tundra like cold of Afghanistan.

I was now physically standing on the soil of Kabul, an ancient city over 3,500 years old that has been the centre stage of many bloody battles fought by great armies. It is believed that Kabul was established between 2000 and 1500 BC. The city is also mentioned as "Kubha" (perhaps meaning Kabul River) in the Rig Veda that was composed between 1700 BC–1100 BC. Even before the invasion of Alexander the Great in 331 BC, Kabul was part of Achaemenid Empire of Persia (BC 553-330) followed by the Seleucid, another Persian Empire of Macedonian Dynasty (BC 323-64). Thereafter it was under the Maurya Empire (BC323-185) of Hindustan (India) that extended from Uzbekistan to Bengal and Tibet to present day Tamil Nadu that was followed by Kushan Empires of Hindustan (India) (BC 130-AD 185). Later the city became part of many more kingdoms before Babur's entry into the city in circa 1504 to become the king of Afghanistan and it is from Kabul in Circa 1519 that Babur launched the campaign against Hindustan to establish the Mughal Empire. He liked Kabul so much that, as per his will, after his death on 26 Jan 1530 in Agra, India, his body was moved to Kabul where it lies in Bagh-e Babur (Babur Gardens) to this day.

I was jolted back to the present reality by the gust of chilling biting into the facial skin that made nose and ears instantly numb and eyes watery. The airport had a desolate look with grey buildings and misty surroundings. As I walked towards the airport building I noticed a dozen or so bearded Afghan Policemen in thick grey uniform carrying Kalashnikov and moving casually around the tarmac. They looked menacing enough to shoot me or anybody without orders, more by default than by design. Having been a stickler for good military discipline and turn out, I was taken aback to see these uniformed men in loose, un-ironed thick fabric grey uniforms with not so smart grey caps that slid backwards showing a puff of unkempt hair on their forehead. They were carrying weapons in different styles, slung over shoulders, dangerously pointing straight ahead ready to shoot, muzzle down and some with muzzle up. Fellow passengers, mostly Indians and Afghans sprinkled with few internationals without smile on their somber faces, walked into what looked like a rough avatar of arrival lounge but first there was the visa check formality to go through. Standing on male line I faced another grey uniformed police man at the visa counter as he took time to scrutinize and stamp my passport. The first experience upon entering the baggage collection lounge was the sight of Afghan porters in dirty white loose fitting salwars, long shirts and dirty jackets or coats, jostling around and pushing huge, strange looking baggage trolleys that had seen better days and I guessed these would be a part of leftover of Russian raj. The smell was dirty, perhaps coming from the long un-bathed bodies of the porters, soldiers and the milieu that were thronging the lounge. Almost everything looked dirty grey whereas the floors were broken cement fragments. The baggage conveyer belt area with its ramshackle broken down pieces of chain looked like ancient abandoned place seen in science fiction movies that suddenly comes to life. Waiting impatiently for the baggage in the congested area, I heard a loud bang and noticed that along with me many people were startled. Expecting trouble I looked around and found that it was the conveyer belt cranked to life by an ancient looking monster of a generator beyond. It kept halting and restarting again and again bringing in luggage in bits and pieces. After much pushing and jostling with the crowd it was a relief to see my 2 suitcases and a golf bag emerging from the small window of the conveyor belt. There were no readily available trolleys taken for granted in all airports of the world but I managed to negotiate with a porter for the services of a broken down trolley he was holding like a private taxi. He demanded a dollar for hiring the trolley but extra 2 dollars for his services. I had no choice but to take this taxi trolley. We loaded the baggage and the porter pushed and pulled the trolley that seemed to function only on 2 wheels making it a struggle along the rough stony pavement outside the airport building. The outer area was more rough and stony and at times the luggage would tumble over. Finally we crossed a police barrier and reached the taxi stand that had many international brands of vehicles including the military and UN SUVs. Although I was told by the company representative before leaving Delhi that there would be a staff with a vehicle to pick me up but I saw none. I asked some drivers in broken Urdu and was told that my reception party could be in the second taxi stand outside gate but that was dangerous place and risky to venture into. Risk or no I had to find my transport so I took a chance and went to the second taxi stand not once but twice with the porter and the imperfect trolley following me but no luck. I borrowed a cellphone from a taxi driver for 1$ and rang up my company and I was told that there was a guy to receive me and his name was Rishad. I asked him the color of jacket or coat Rashid was wearing and was told that it was a red jacket. I searched and searched the length and breadth of both the taxi stands and finally noticed a red jacket far away near the entrance gate of the building. I yelled "Rishad" and he instantly reacted by turning around and waving his hand much to my relief and his. Instead of writing my name or company name in a piece of paper to display at the exit gate the company guy had given Rishad an enlarged copy of my first page passport that had me wearing a shirt and tie with scanty hair combed over whereas my current avatar was a bald head with a French beard to balance. It is lack of common sense on such a minor issue but common sense is not always common in many parts of the world.

The driver was pleasant looking handsome, medium statured Afghan in a worn out brown leather jacket and faded jeans who welcomed me with a pleasant smile and "Salam alleikum" as he opened the car door. I was immediately relaxed when the driver switched on the car music system and Bollywood song of Kishore Kumar, *"Jiwan ke Safar Men Rahi"* filled the space. It was a pleasant surprised and when I asked him, he replied in Hindi, "Janab, I have seen more Hindi Movies than you may have". I felt good and secure. As he drove along, I looked through the car window and noticed lines of unevenly spread mud houses and few concrete buildings. It reminded me of villages in Punjab way back in the early 60s. Punjab is now a highly developed and rich state with its villages lined with bungalows, thanks to the green revolution and the flow of foreign currencies from Punjabi expats.

I wondered why there was no color in Kabul, why almost everything was grey or mud colored. As we drove further into Kabul I noticed the country side was dotted with mud houses that almost matched the harshness of barren

Mud Houses along the way

Hindu Kush. The company was located about 10 kms from the airport along Jalalabad road that runs south west from Kabul towards Pakistan. The roads were muddy and wet with recent winter rains matching the cold weather and the dullness of the place. Wheeling left from the highway along the Jalalabad Road we came across Armored vehicles, tanks and Humvees of ISAF (International Security Assistance Force) patrolling the roads, "Clear and Present Danger" was almost palpable here.

We crossed the UN compound that had blue UN flag fluttering in the cold wind and noticed the entire area barricaded by huge walls topped by double rows of Razor Blade double concertina coil fencing and heavily guarded entrance gate. Along the way I could see clusters of houses, offices, stores made of huge containers. Use of huge shipping containers as a readymade housing solution all over Kabul was common. It was because regular flow of aid materials from outside world to Afghanistan in these containers that came to Karachi by sea thereafter by land route via Pakistan to Afghanistan.

All these clusters were inside barbed wire perimeter fencing with gates manned by Kalashnikov wielding uniformed private Security Guards.

The driver turned left leaving the Jalalabad Road and entered a dirt track that lead to the company.

Company Gate As we approached the company premises a heavy iron gate slid open to let us in. Unlike the unclean world outside the cleanliness of the compound and buildings gave me a pleasant surprise. It was the compound of a US-Afghan Multi National Company that manufactured beverage. There were barrack like buildings in neat rows, mostly under construction and renovation. Only one building towards the right side of the gate seemed to be ready and functioning. That was the office building. Inside the building I was received by a young man with oriental looks, being used to living with my troops from the North East India I asked him if he was a Manipuri. I guessed he understood my question as he told me that he was a Filipino. Across a clean corridor I was shown to a well polished teak paneled door with brass "Conference" plate on it. Upon entering I found a group of people seated on black leathered executive swivel chairs around a long conference table. The group looked a mix of Asians and Europeans. Seated on the head of the table was a smart looking middle-aged man with typical El Pacino look, that was Mike the Greek General Manager; next to him on the right side was a heavy built white man with blue eyes and shining bald plate, Ken Waugh, the Australian Director of operations. I was ushered into a vacant chair next to the Australian. Rest looked all Asians and the one seated opposite me had south Indian written all over his face! That was Praful Bhaskaran, the National Sales manager who became my best buddy cum cooking partner in months to come. Next to him was another South Indian, Ramesh, Praful's assistant. A steaming hot mug of coffee materialized that was the most welcome thing ever since I landed in Kabul. I was welcomed and introduced to the team by the affable "El Pacino" on whose left was Mehtab Ahmed the Pakistani Finance Manager and next to Mehtab were Ibrahim, another Pakistani Warehouse Manager. The remaining people were Indian, Pakistani and Philipino supervisors and staff. After the conference Mike and Ken showed me around the company premises, factory, assembly line, warehouse, personnel quarters and I made a mental note of work to be done on security front. However, there was much to be seen and done, such as guest houses, routes, marketing areas, liaison with the police, army and UN for security feeds. Besides, paper work was to be done in the form of writing SOPs (Standard Operating Procedures) on the security & safety of factories, guest houses, ware houses, movement of personnel of the company. What I was looking at now was only the tip of the iceberg.

On hind sight, as I look back it was a challenge to be in charge of security in Afghanistan. At that time real danger and everyday threat posed to human lives never struck me. It was another job, another security issue to tackle, albeit in a very different environment. However, I had to understand and digest that here in Afghanistan although Taliban was out but not down and it was regularly raising its ugly head in the form of terror attacks in its areas of choosing. Far from it they were still intact and operating with impunity from their safe haven in Pakistan. I was not going to be dealing with security threat to bank branches from Naxals in remote areas in India but here I was up against Taliban terrorists with state of art weapon and communication systems spread across the country and the world. They remained in the shadows and struck unexpectedly only to merge in the shadows again.

By evening we wrapped up and headed to the guest house that was located on the other end of Kabul in a place called Karte-Se. I was driven across the Kabul city to the guest house and I was not surprised at the site of Kabul after so many years of war and devastation. The city in the dim street lights looked quite primitive with dirty streets generally wet due to recent winter rains, buildings on either side of the road were dull looking, either grey or mud colored houses and few buildings. We passed a small hill full of mud houses. The first group of concrete buildings I saw was rows of grey stone and cement buildings in not so clean surroundings. That, I was told by the driver was "Makriyon" the Russian built government quarters. The traffic was right hand and the vehicles were left hand driven, slightly awkward to adjust initially. There were numerous stalls with huge carcass of beef on sale; smoke puffing road side vendors cooking and selling Kebabs and children pushing wheelbarrows filled with mixed utility items on sale. There were also road side

vendors waving wads of Afghan currency notes for foreign exchange. I saw beggars along the roadside, some in burqua and quite many in crutches with stumps of leg dangling, obviously the victims of war and numerous land mines planted during the last 30 years. What struck me as strange was that despite 4 years of ouster of Taliban and establishment of the new government, I could not see any visible signs of reconstruction. Kabul looked like an old, beat up and destroyed city just about limping

Kabul Streets-Sloshed and Jammed

back to life at this time of the day. I came to understand later that Kabul had no power source and the whole city was partially illuminated by generators. Strange, even after 4 years of international presence the basic infrastructure for human need is not available.

After driving for about an hour we reached a small market area that was called "Karte-Se" and another 5 minutes drive along another dirty road the driver wheeled right towards a black painted tall gate that opened to a big double storey building. This was our guest house. I was welcomed by a Nepali boy, who was the cook cum manager, the one and only staff of the guest house where 6 Indian staff were housed. I was the 7th one. The lounge and the dining areas were tastefully done with rich polished furniture, TV and music system. I was led out of the backdoor of the drawing room into a huge courtyard with garden and lawn. Across the lawn was a big outhouse, an annex that was to be my home. As I entered the main door, it opened into a small corridor, which lead to a spacious and well-furnished drawing room with a dining table with chairs. On the other side was a bed room. Both had diesel operated heaters locally called "Bhukari". It kept the room reasonably warm. During dinner all gathered in the dining room and I was introduced to all the residents. There were Praful and Ramesh, the sales heads, Hakim and Nasim, beverage technicians from Mumbai and Kutty Nair, electrical supervisor from Mumbai. Nice guys in quest of better dollar based Eldorado in Afghanistan. All of them had worked in the Middle East before and only the better package brought them to Kabul. I hit it off instantly with Praful; after all, he was the son of a colonel. After introduction and chitchat Praful asked me for a drink and I said why not. He had beer and I had brandy with warm water, my favorite during winters. Dinner was Uzbek Pulao, very richly cooked rice with raisin and "Dumba" (Afghan sheep) which is half fat and half red meat. It was fatty, sweet but tasty. As I was hungry after long travel and only coffee in office I wolfed it down with vengeance. Night was cold and in spite of well-made bed with good blankets I chose to sleep in my alpine sleeping bag.

Next morning after quick bath and breakfast of omelet and parathas served by the ever smiling Nepali boy, I was picked up by the company Terracan SUV at 7.30 am. Early morning drive through the streets of Kabul in a cold day was a pleasant experience. People had started going about their work. Houses & eateries were puffing with smoke, shops were opening and traffic was coming alive. Now I noticed bullet marks on the walls of many houses, streets were dirty and garbage littered along the sideways. However, also along the dirt and destruction there were bits and pieces of beautiful Kabul of yore. There were beautiful cherry trees lining the streets and patches of gardens and lawns along the roads and intersections. Long ago some wise people had taken pains to plant such beautiful trees along the roadside that would provide shade and bear fruit as well as flower. These had survived the vagaries of weather and war. Wheelbarrow vendors were coming out for their small business and pushing their Russian carts to the designated places along the streets, butchers shops were opening with beef and dumba carcass being hung at the shop windows and the smoke of kebabs from roadside eateries had started wafting through the streets filling the morning air with delicious aroma. We drove through the city crossed the main highway and entered Jalalabad Road and finally reached the gate of the company that was opened by the guards. This is how my work and stay in Kabul started.

Kabul of my Imagination

My early knowledge of Afghanistan was of the 1950s when a group of very stately and handsome Afghan Prince were suddenly seen in Kalimpong, our small hometown in the Eastern Himalayan foothills. We were told that these alien people were the Afghan Royals exiled from their homeland. We saw them walking from their home in the Durpin Hills to town, a distance of about 4-5 kms. They were stately, elegant and beautiful and kept to themselves. We never saw them talking with locals or outsiders. My next experience was Hindi movie, "Kabuliwala", a classic master piece made by Bimal Roy with Balraj Sahni as the main lead. The story is based on an Afghan from Kabul, "Kabuliwala", comes to Kolkata to do business and gets very attached to a Bengali family and their little girl who reminds him of his own little daughter back home. He later gets implicated in a crime and serves a life sentence in jail. Upon release he finds that the little girl of the Bengali family has now grown up and getting married. The last scene is the Kabuliwala returning back to Kabul on a camel back and visualising his little daughter to be the same little girl he had left behind many years ago. That was Afghanistan and Kabul for me. However, over the years, I had closely followed with interest the series of turmoil in Afghanistan, the coups, revolts, Russian occupation, Taliban's atrocities and finally the US invasion and installation of present Government.

Kabul in 2006

What Kabul went through; after the royal Coup in 1973, ousting a gentleman King, Zahir Shah, the civil war, Soviet occupation and more civil war and the final downfall of Taliban in 2001, is a part of history and there is nothing anyone can do to change the past. However, in spite of international outrage and much hyped efforts to rebuild and modernize the country by the international community I did not see any visible work of reconstruction in the city. All that was visible was massive movement of ISAF and UN Vehicles, huge barricaded compounds of International companies and rows and rows of cargo tankers all over the city.

Part of Kabul

Tank Barrel over mud houses

I did not see electricity generation and distribution system, good roads, flyovers, modern public transportation systems. It was quite surprising that the one and only international airport of Kabul still struggled to function in its old structure. There was no visibility of basic modern comfort including a descent toilet or lounge. Kabul functioned on imported generators in all dwellings, shops, offices and malls. The only modernization noticeable was number of malls with European brands that were primarily meant for the affluent. I would have loved to see massive plantation drive in the city and a functional garbage disposable system. I would also have loved to see the historic Kabul river cleaned and fresh water flowing through it with lines of trees on both the banks. Sadly, the legendary river trickling through the city was still black with city's waste and excreta. There were big places like the Kabul Serena Hotel of Agha Khan Group, The Intercontinental Hotel, both 5 Star properties that continued to be targets of Taliban attacks. The roads were potholed, dirty; the municipal garbage disposal did not seem to exist. When it rained the muck and slush dominated the roads of the city. Most importantly, there was no electricity and the entire city was illuminated by high powered generators imported from UK, Germany, and France etc. These were huge diesel generators that were designed to run nonstop for months. In other words reconstructions work; if any that brought immediate relief to the public was not visible at all and in any case not in public view. Postal system did not exist.

Living and working in the city for a year, I had the privilege to watch from close quarters and experience the unique Afghan life as also the lives of so many people from other countries.

Kabul Street scene

It was enriching to interact with many people from different nations who lived and worked in the city. There were many private security companies of different western nations who were doing brisk business selling security arrangements to international corporations, NGOs business houses etc. Security with its doomsday predicting marketing managers was a thriving business in the city. Owned and operated by veterans of US, UK and other Western nations these companies were manned by veterans drawing handsome packages; after all they were risking their lives for pure greenback dollars. I came across security managers who were veterans from US, UK, France, and Germany. The grounds men guards were mostly from the Gorkha Regiment veterans from Nepal's British Army and Indian Army. They were also recruiting and training Afghan youths for the job. However, it was surprising that a private company could also engage Afghan Police Guards on payment. My company had engaged few such policemen and I found that it was a good idea to do so and to be on the right side of relationship with the police. The Police officer of the local police station used to come to the company regularly to check the police guards. It fell upon me to engage him during such visits. Surprisingly he started becoming overfriendly and even gave hints of certain needs for his family. Later he told me that he was unwell and wanted to go to Delhi for medical checkup and if he could stay at my home during such a visit. I told him that I live in Eastern part of India in the Himalayan foothills very far away from Delhi. In a war torn capital city under the constant threat of bomb blasts, firing, kidnaping and murder, security industry ought to do well.

Street Hookah Bar & Demolished Taliban Camp near Golf Course

Weather- Heat, Dust & Snow

Early morning of 1ˢᵗ January 2006, when I opened my eyes and pulled the curtains from the French window next to my bed, I was greeted by a beautiful sight of soft looking snowflakes falling all over the courtyard that had bathed the entire lawn and garden in pure whiteness. I got up from the bed and stepped out of the house in woolen pajamas, woolen dressing gown and slippers, while hugging myself against the snowy morning chill. I found the lawn, garden, roof, the trees and everything buried under fresh snow. I look up and find the sky is seamless blue and the snow so white that my eyes dazzle and burn. I step inside my room and feel the warmth emitted by the cast iron diesel stove that glows nonstop. It was my first snow fall in Kabul on the first day of the year. Situated at 5,876 feet in a valley astride Kabul River and hemmed in the foothills of Hindu Kush mountain ranges, Kabul has semi-arid climate but inside the snowbelt. It has harsh winter with snow fall that has temperature going below zero between December to February. Springs in March- April are pleasant and also the wettest time of the year with regular rains that makes slushy and murky roads. By May it is hot and dusty and frequented by dust and sand storm. Once the snow solidifies, the streets are slippery and cold. It is pathetic to see very poor, young children and elderly people begging in the streets, wearing scanty, torn clothing against the harsh cold weather. Some of them would huddle over a bonfire of thrown cardboards, papers and packing material to keep them warm albeit for a while.

December Sunset after Snowfall

What would be their condition in the cold nights is anybody's imagination. The Russian built Makriyon Housing colony for government staff had water heaters through pipelines for the entire colony. Every shop, government offices or private companies or affluent class had diesel operated heaters in their homes and offices. It is the poor all over the world who suffer the vagaries of weather. Come summer by June-July, heat and dust would take over the ancient capital.

Melting Pot of Humanity

I found Kabul to be a melting pot of people from many nations; as such, it was a unique experience to be part of this diverse multinational, multiethnic and multilingual population that had come to Kabul seeking their part of Eldorado. There were many NGOs at work towards nation building. There were builders from Turkey, Iran, Greece and security companies from USA, UK France, Germany and manpower companies from Nepal. There were business houses run by Non Resident Afghans who lived in US, Europe and Middle East and most of them operated from Dubai, a safer haven just two hours flying time. There were work force from India, Pakistan, Sri Lanka, Philippine and Nepal who also came to Kabul to make a living. Just like the legacy of history, when people like Alexander the Great, Hordes of Genghis Khan, Timur the Lame and Babur walked on the soil of Kabul, even today it is a melting pot of people from different hues. The population of the city reflects the general multi-ethnic and multi-lingual characteristics of Afghanistan. The city is home to Tajiks, Hazaras, Pashtuns, Uzbeks, Baluch, Turkmen, Iranian, Iraqis, Arabs and in present time people from almost all over the world. When I carefully studied the features of Uzbeks men and women, I noticed their resemblance to the Macedonians.

They were handsome, tall, fair, blue eyed with chiseled faces and sculpted bodies. No doubt that Uzbeks, in physical appearance, are one of the most beautiful people on earth. Uzbek women are so beautiful that would leave all the Miss Universes and Miss World's miles behind. Languages spoken in the city are Dari (Afghan Persian) and Pashto although Dari is de-facto lingua franca. Nearly all the people of Kabul are Muslims, which includes the majority Sunnis and minority Shias. A small number of Sikhs, Hindus, and Christians are also found in the city as permanent citizens from times immemorial. However, history tells us that Islamisation made inroads to Kabul only in 7th century AD when the first Islamic dynasty was established in 870 AD. The Rig-Veda mentions Kabul as a beautiful city like a vision of

Ex-Mujahedeen on way to surrender arsenals to UN

paradise in the lap of mountains. It was a part of Hindu civilisation from the beginning that later became home to Zoroastrianism, Buddhism but Hinduism continued. Presently, there is a large number of floating multinational population. The ethnic population of Kabul has fluctuated since the early 1980s. It was around 500,000 in 2001 but after the fall of Taliban many self-exiled Afghans returned home, primarily from Pakistan and Iran. By 2009, the population was little over 3.5 million. This includes a large population from other provinces that stay in Kabul on temporary basis for jobs as well as to escape the fighting in the provinces. I was blessed enough to visit one and only Hindu Mandir in area Karte-Se where a "Diya" (Oil Lamp) burns permanently. It is a huge structure in a private compound of the temple amazingly left untouched by the Taliban. Besides the people from the West who worked in the UN, NGOs, Security Agencies or managing their own business and construction companies there were nationals from countries like India, Pakistan, Nepal, Philippine, Turkey, Srilanka, Bangladesh working in UN, various projects, business, hotels and restaurants. Few from Bhutan were found only in the UN but the Nepalese were everywhere. Bars and restaurants had girls from Nepal at reception and there were fairly big populations of Nepalese working in security agencies, hotels, bars and UN canteens. Some were enterprising enough running manpower and security business. I met a young boy at Kabul airport who had the air ticket to go back home to Nepal but not even 10 USD to pay the airport fees. I paid that amount and told him to go home straight.

Kabuliwalas and their Ways

Moving around the city and its outskirts I found many Afghans, Tajiks, Uzbeks and Hazaras, whether officials, shop keepers, business men, rich, poor, middle class, friendly and amenable. None of these people carried ego baggage. Of many high and middle level officials I met, no one had that superior egoistic air about them that Indian bureaucracy is loaded with. As for few women staff I interacted they were all normal human beings, not at all shying away from men as perceived by many. They would go about their work like any other women of the world. I came across nurses and cleaning staff in the hospitals but never saw an Afghan lady doctor. The impact of misogynist Taliban rule had left visible scars. In the city's shopping complexes I saw girls mostly in groups or in company of other men but never alone. There was not a single girl as a shop keeper. I was reminded of India's North Easter States like Mizoram, Nagaland and Meghalaya, where women run almost all the shops and bargain tough to the point of telling the customer "Take it or leave it". I used to visit a tailor shop in a small market near my guest house; he always offered me Afghan black tea. One day I found it was gutted by electric fire. He narrated the incident with sadness but still offered me the usual tea. When I gave him $100 to help rebuild his shop he was so touched that he held my hand and kissed it and called me brother. Another florist shop keeper told me that he was saving money to get married as the bridegroom had to pay a huge sum to the bride's family before the marriage. I thought of the contrast in my country where a girl's family has to pay astronomical amount to the bridegroom's family and numerous cases of domestic violence and dowry deaths of young innocent girls.

Like everywhere in the world, there are romances and love affairs. A young procurement staff of my company in his early twenties used to confide in me about his girlfriend and that he was always in pins and needles whether she would be able to receive his calls. It turned out that they were distant relatives who met in a marriage and fell in love. He also told me that he longed to hold his beloveds hands someday. I could also see the building up of love affair between our beautiful, smart and well educated twenty something receptionist Noor and a smart, handsome cleaner boy, Afzal. They became little bold by Afghan standard and started spending time in the office and canteen together. Obviously it was not very good for the management as such they were expelled from the job. She was devastated to lose her job and came crying to me. I helped her find a job in a bank through a known friend.

Later, when I met her again she told me crying that her boyfriend had ditched her and got married with another girl. They were all normal human beings, young people who fell in and out of love like any other young people of the world. There was another case of a very beautiful Uzbek woman who came to join our company as a cleaner. She was recommended for the job as she had married a 60 plus amputee with many children and had to work to look after the new family. Obviously, it looked like a forced sacrifice. What we used to read and hear about 70-80 year old men marrying teenagers is a fact of life in Afghanistan specially so in the rural areas. Some of our staff members used to invite me during marriages or religious festivals where I found myself seated with elderly menfolk of the house on beautiful carpets spread on the ground with matching pillows and bolsters in Mughals style. In such occasions the first serve used to be coke and sweetened watermelon, perhaps as an appetizer that used to be followed by sumptuous and very rich Uzbek Pulao floating in ghee, sheep meat and raisin accompanied by varieties of kababs and huge giant size nan or tandoori roti (bread). Tasteless black tea after the meal was customary but having got used to my own brand of Darjeeling tea, it used to be quite an agony for me to push Afghan tea down my throat. No women ever came out to the drawing room to meet the guests and food used to be served by the young men of the family. Only once, when I was invited to the home of a lady staff, all the family members including old and young ladies came out to greet me. They sat around chatted with me in broken Urdu and English and shared coke and sweetened melon as also insisted on taking photos with me while placing their hands on my shoulders. Exceptions prove the rule. This was an educated westernized family who had spent years in Iran during the Taliban rule.

Perhaps due to proximity and old links many Afghans frequented Pakistan and Iran as a way of life. I was quite surprised that for major ailments like surgery, the not so affluent would go to Pakistan but affluent ones chose India's Delhi, Mumbai or Bangalore as their medical destination. A driver of my company, who came on the way of Taliban bomb blast receiving serious burns, was sponsored by the company for treatment in All India Institute of Medical Sciences in Delhi that put him back to shape. The barber shop I visited to trim my hair and beard had signboard with Bollywood actor Sanjay Dutt and Preity Zinta and a friendly young barber who worked on me was always full of Bollywood songs, humming along while working his craft. The first thing that struck me when I roamed the streets of Kabul was many hoardings of Bollywood actress Katrina Kaif on "Alkozey Tea" advertisement.

She was almost everywhere, highways, city streets, intersections. There were posters of many other actors and actresses all over the city mostly on advertisement of jewelry, garments, electronic goods etc.

My Work at a Glance

To fathom the kind of security threat in Afghanistan it may be sufficient to understand the mindset of a suicide bomber ***Mohammed Al-Ghoul,*** who said, ***"How beautiful it is to kill or to be killed.........for the lives of the coming generations".***

A collage of Human Bombs (Courtesy Google)

As Security Chief my first task was to establish a compact security system in the company that encompassed security of personnel and company resources. The security of personnel was complex as the task meant providing a 100 plus multinational, multiethnic and multicultural people from very different back ground at work, residence and importantly during movement. However, the first thing was the physical security of the company and guest houses. Luckily, after few days of my joining, the company gave me a very able, spirited, proactive and a lovable guy from the Philippines as my deputy. He was ex Police sergeant in his country and he was an expert on electronic security, a subject quite new to me. So first I made a security plan for the company that encompassed the offices, the factory, living quarters of guards and kitchen staff. Since the entire Kabul was in danger zone I did not have to waste time on prioritizing the danger areas. I made computer sketch of the security plan including CCTV plan, discussed with management staff and concerned departmental heads and finalized it and got the work started. The plan had perimeter walls with razor blade concertina double apron fencing, security lights, and watch towers with guard posts. Guards were recruited and trained for which elaborate training schedules were prepared that included Security Standard Operating Procedures, Emergency Security Procedures and Fire Procedures.

The same procedure was followed for the residential areas of guest houses. The most important and difficult was the security of personnel during their movement from the house to the company and vice versa. Besides, there had to be a separate Standing Operating Procedures for the Sales and Marketing managers as they had to undertake extensive movement across the city for their daily work. There were innumerable contingencies that had to be visualised and procedures prepared and explained to every person of the company.

Weapon Handling Procedures: Another important issue for the security staff was the Standard Operating Procedures for weapon handling. For the ease of their understanding I divided this in two parts, First; Basic Weapon Safety and Second; Rules of weapon engagement. In the Safety aspects the points elaborated were; firstly, to treat all weapons as loaded, secondly, always point weapons towards the safe direction that is if fired by accident it would not harm any person, thirdly, keep fingers away from the trigger and fourthly, always identify the target and check background. In the aspect of weapon handling the factors stressed to the staff were; first, to ensure normal safety precautions while receiving or handing over a weapon, second, to carry weapon at all times and not to leave it in the vehicle or anywhere, third, clean weapon after duty in a separate designated area and fourth, to remember the state of weapon all the time.

The ultimate factor of the whole security system was the use of fire arms most effectively. That meant very detailed instructions and training to open fire for effect but before that it was the correct identification of the target in terms of attacker, whether a terrorist, a Taliban attacker or a simple thief or robber. There were Government rules and regulation for possessing and opening fire by a civilian in self defense. For that purpose license and arms registration was required. We could buy weapons without much problem but using the weapon against another human being whether to kill or hurt was another matter and every firing had to be covered under self defense.

Dealing with Human Bombs: The new found terrorist strategy of Human Bombs (Person Bearing Explosives-PBE) had been gaining momentum and there were instances of such strategy being employed in Afghanistan. After much deliberations and research I finally wrote a crisp Aide Memoir on this subject as under:-

First was to understand the behaviour of a Person Borne Explosive (Male or Female). The general behavior of a person carrying explosives on his/her body could be as under:-

- Sweating
- Mumbling, possibly praying
- Recently clean shaven
- Looking anxious
- Wearing bulky clothing not in keeping with the weather or event
- Holding something in the hand / clenched fist
- Wire or toggle protruding from overtly carried bag

The Principle of 6 Cs in Dealing with Human Bombs: It is vital that no one takes immediate action so as to alert the PBE and impending actions by Army or Police may be compromised. So follow the principal of 6 Cs:-

- Confirm- description of the suspect
- Cover- that is withdraw about 50 yards but maintain discreet visual contact
- Contact-superiors or Police
- Civilians-in the vicinity, direct them to other areas without raising suspicion

- Colleagues- Prevent other security staff from entering in to this area

- Check- for other suspects or devices

We organised special training session for the entire company personnel on this subject as I felt that awareness of such vital issues was a step towards the right direction.

With Deputy & Security Staff

In my course of duty I interviewed many male and female Afghans for various posts and ruthlessly selected the fit ones while rejecting the unfit, especially those who came armed with connections and recommendations. In one such interview for the post of a security supervisor the interviewee claimed to have been the radio operator of the legendary Leader and commander of the Northern Alliance, Ahmad Shah Massoud. As he took his seat, this man displayed extreme deliberation in placing his shades and two cell phones on the table and started talking to the lady translator with much interest. However, he could not answer my simple questions on ground level security duties. I looked into his eyes and told him that he was unfit for the post under consideration and told him to leave. Expecting a sure shot employment because of name dropping there was shock and disbelief on his face. So was the case in selection of security equipment vendor when I had to select a lesser known, poor but hard working vendor against a rich Germany based vendor connected with one of the investors. He came to the office and demanded to know why he was not selected, I showed the carefully made comparative statement of all the vendors where his price was highest and quality questionable. He left without a word and no question was asked by the management.

Interesting Places in Kabul

In spite of long decades of civil war and the devastation it caused, there are still historic sights worth experiencing in Kabul. Amongst many interesting landmarks what struck me most Darul Aman Palace, Wall of Bones and the unique golf course, the one and only in Afghanistan. They are divergently different but aroused a kind of special interest in me.

Darul Aman Palace: The old battered palace stood like an edifice of another world, a huge structure in complete ruins yet exhibiting a rich legacy of the yore. It stood tall amongst its own ruins, the tall walls, the broken roof and the skeletons of the once towering domes. It was as if giving a message to the universe that it would rise from its ashes just like the phoenix. It was while reconnoitering a route for marathon race, to be held in the city for the first time after 26 years, I came across this ruins of this majestic palace about 20 kms west of Kabul. Darul Aman, meaning "abode of peace" was built by king Anamullah in early 1920s. He was a forward looking and modern monarch and brought many reforms in his kingdom that was a fiercely tribal and feudal society. His reforms included electricity for the city and schooling for girls, a major step in a region that was almost misogynist in its outlook. The palace was an opulence of grace and beauty with its high domes, gardens, fountains amidst lush green lawns. However, unfortunately, the fate of this beautiful palace got intertwined with the fate of the country that became epicenter of civil war and many battles engulfing the beauty of this palace in its unending flames of violence trampling human lives, art, culture and nature.

Darul Aman Palace - Original Glory

Darul Aman Palace - Present Ruins

The end game for the palace started in 1929 when the King had to leave Kabul due to a local uprising under Habibullah Kalakani. However, within few months Kalakani was executed by Nader Khan who proclaimed himself the king and occupied the palace. The new king was also assassinated soon thereafter leaving the throne to his 19-year-old son, Zahir Shah who became the King of Afghanistan in in 1933. Over the next 40 years King Zahir Shah ruled the country and modernized and liberalised it to a great extent.

In 1973 when the king was visiting Europe his cousin Daoud Khan who served as Prime Minister took over as the self-declared President backed by Russia. This episode opened the floodgates of civil war and strife that tore the beautiful country over the next three decade and continues till today albeit in the dimension of terrorism. While walking around the ruins of the palace I saw the rubbles caused by many years of bombings and thousands of bullet marks all over the walls. The once beautiful domes had caved in leaving only the part of the superstructure with gaping holes. I stood there in wonder that in spite of being a battlefield over three decades, part of the palace, specially many walls and superstructure of the roof still stood erect, as if defying the violence and destruction it was subjected to over a prolonged period of history. Sadly, what started as a majestic landmark symbol of peace and prosperity in the kingdom of Afghanistan and the entire region, ended as an ugly symbol of senseless human violence. Once beautiful gardens, lush green lawns and ever flowing fountains are now covered by rows and rows of graveyard of people that are decorated by litter and animal or human wastes. I understand the present government plans to restore the palace to its original glory. I hope and pray that happens soon enough in the near future and that would encourage many people like me to take another trip to Kabul so as to see Darul Aman palace in its original beauty and glory.

Wall of Bones: Another ruin of the yore that fascinated me was the Great Wall of Kabul nick named "Wall of Bones". It runs atop the Sher Darwaza (Lion's Door) mountains, towering over the city below. It is believed that the wall was built by King Zamburak Shah in the sixth century so as to keep out Muslim invaders. Zamburak was a cruel ruler who used to force all male subjects to labor to build this wall. It is rumored that those who refused or became sick or too old to work were killed and their bones were meshed into the wall.

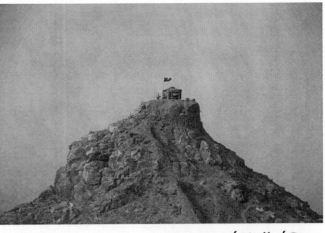

A section of Wall of Bones

It is also believed that one day, when the King was visiting the wall, he was attacked and killed by his workers and his bones were also buried in the wall. The present Government, after finding some bones in the walls has sent them for scientific evaluation which may bring out the truth. The Kabul Municipality has started a project of making the area of the wall a fruit orchard. A great step forward towards rebuilding the once beautiful. *"People are ashamed of what has happened to their city and the fact the world only thinks of war when they see Afghanistan. We want to rebuild these palaces exactly as they were before."* says the city mayor who is appreciated for the herculean task he has taken up towards major plantation drive and road repairs. Good luck to him and his noble venture.

Kabul Golf Course: The Most Dangerous Golf Course in the World: Can any golfer imagine playing golf with a pistol tugged under his belt and a shot gun in the golf bag along with wood and iron clubs? Not because he is a wanabe Rambo but because there is a serious and genuine threat from Taliban that a golfer could be shot at or ambushed/ abducted. That is Kabul Golf Course, the one and only in Afghanistan. Being an avid golfer when I learnt about this golf course I took the first opportunity on a Friday weekend to find the place and play there. Also on the way to the Golf course I crossed Taliban's camp area that was raised to the ground by invading NATO forces. About 10 kms from Kabul, the golf course is located adjacent to scenic Quargah Lake and Park adorned with blooming flowers, a beautiful picnic spot. The golf hut affords a beautiful and close view of the lake with emerald green water.

Golfing during weekend Truce

The shore is dotted with beautiful picnic huts built on small platform with Mughal style canopy and curtains for privacy. Visitors enjoy motorboats rides but swimming is prohibited as I learnt that few people who tried to swim towards the center of the lake never came back for reasons unknown.

The golf course, it is best described in the words of a **"one page brochure"** issued by the club, its "Tips" and general instructions are quoted as hereunder, copied word to word:-

"Welcome to the Kabul Golf Course, the best and only golf course in Afghanistan. This is a desert style course where 18 Tee Boxes play to 9 Holes. Begin your, round with a dramatic tee shot from high ground over the valley below. Be sure to bring a camera and get a trophy photograph of yourself teeing off because your friends will never believe that you played golf in Afghanistan".

Golf Restaurant Billboard riddled with Bullets

The Fairway

"Attack the course! Play aggressively. There are no gimmes. This is golf with an attitude".

"Wear long trousers and shocks for protection from desert plants. Lockers and showers are not available, but you can go jump in the lake for free" and for refreshments, "Players should bring a bottle of water for while on the course".

"Players who have never been on a desert style course up in the mountain are in for a surprise. The Kabul Golf Club will challenge you with sand, dust that's sometimes packed into hard pan and plants and wild life of all kinds. The course reward precision shots, and to be successful you'll need to use the special techniques described below"

"Caddie – It's difficult to find your ball in the sand and rocks of the desert course and the drives go longer in the high altitude and dry air. So you'll need a bag caddie to carry your clubs up and down the hill and also a fore caddie who will run forward to spot where your ball lands. When is the last time you enjoyed such a luxury?"

"Rough play", "On a desert course, rough is really rough, the idea is simple, from the fairway you can use a Tee but from the rough you can't"

"Water Hazard", "You'll find one of these on the course although it is dry. So use your imagination and treat it in the normal way. If your ball lands on it, even though you can actually play the shot, it's deemed unplayable and a penalty and a drop must be taken. Look at it like this; you can retrieve your ball without getting wet. What more do you want?

"Browns", "The green are browns made from oil and sand which is compacted to provide a smooth surface. The speed of your ball will be much slower on browns than greens, but then again you can read the break easier because balls leave a trail on the sand"

"The Gallery": "Afghans like sports and are curious about golf, most having seen it only on TV. The Kabul Golf Course is built along a road leading to a popular park, so don't be surprised when cars and buses stop and cause a traffic jam so passengers can watch you play and take photographs. It is not unheard of for a gallery to collect and follow a flight from hole to hole, applauding for their favorite player. Just enjoy being a celebrity and wave politely as if this happens every time you play. Then try not to flub your next shot. Good Luck

It is the only golf course in the world where it is perfectly normal for a golfer to carry a weapon. In fact when I played for the first time it had been de-mined by US Army Engineers and I played in a foursome with US and Greek Army Officers. All of us carried our pistols under the belt at the small of the back and felt quite comfortable with it. The shot gun found a slot in the golf bag. As mentioned in the brochure the fairways were so rough and stony that we had to use Tee or mat. The course was quite challenging in the sense that the first tee off from the top of the hill to valley below, 3rd was across the main road hidden away in a slope that had to be approached from the top side, the 4th had to be reached through fairway of boulders and rocks while the 5th hole was atop a steep hill that shot had to be well calibrated to get to the brown or its apron. More often than not our balls would hit the rocks or stones on the fairway and bounce haywire but the caddies were used to it and could spot the balls much to our relief.

Golfing with a 9 mm Beretta under the belt, just in case

The History of the Course: It was in 1911 that king Emir Hajibullah brought golf to Afghanistan by building this Course. It is said that the king spent much time in the course that people started placing their petitions into the holes at night so that it could have the king's attention while putting into the hole the next morning. It is also believed that golf was such a passion for him that after assassination in 1919 his body was buried near a golf course in Jalalabad. It may be logical to assume that instead of RIP the king's grave could have had the epitaph of GIP (Golf in Peace).

The Kabul Golf Club thrived till 1973 after which it was disturbed due coups and civil war. After the Soviet occupation of the country in 1979 the fortune of the club further dwindled as tanks were rolling along the fairway and the course came under heavy crossfire between Soviet troops and

Quargah Lake & Garden adjacent to Golf Course

Mujahedeen. Interestingly the power and *lure* of the game was so much that weekly truce was agreed upon between the Soviet Army and Mujahedeen fighters so that embassy officials and Kabul golfers could play during the weekends. The Kabul Golf Club thus became a legend as the most dangerous golf course on earth. With the departure of the Soviets in 1989, the course was strewn with dangerous litter of war. Permitting only volleyball in long pants, Taliban had put an end to whatever was left of the course and also mined the fairways. It was only in 2004 that the course was declared mine free and opened once again. That is how I was able to play in 2006 and to commemorate my fun time in the world's most dangerous golf course, as remembrance, I bought a Second hand 400 cc Hippo Driver from the club pro, Abdul for 20 USD that I use to this day most happily. I would fail in my duties towards Kabul Golf Club if I did not mention about the brave Pro, Mr Mohammad Afzal Abdul - "Abdul".

"Abdul" the Pro

Baby Caddie

He is the club's teaching pro, manager, bar tender, public relations director as also sometimes, a dishwasher, handyman and greens keeper. His golf life began at the age of 8 when an American gave him a 5 Iron. He loves and respects the golf so much that during the Russian occupation when he found tanks in the fairway he told the Russian officers to remove the tanks from the course. On his repeated insistence the Russians got bored and put him in the jail for 6 months. After his release he went to Kashmir to become a taxi driver, from caddie to a cabbie! After the war when he returned he found that Taliban also had no interest in golf. When he told Taliban to leave the golf course alone they also put him in jail. After release he went back to Kashmir and bid his time driving taxi for living. Finally, after the fall of Taliban he was able to return to his beloved country and golf course and started rebuilding again. This is how golf lovers are able to play golf in the world's most dangerous golf course.

A Screened seating in Quargah Garden

Samarkand the International Watering Hole

There are few watering holes in Kabul for quenching thirst of international community. The one I liked the most was "Samarkand", a restaurant and bar with living accommodation that belonged to an Uzbek landlord. It was a beautiful property of 3 storey old style stone building with stone floors and small windows. There was a large garden with lush green lawn dotted with mulberry trees which, during the spring, used to bow down with juicy fruits painting the tree violet. There was a fountain at the center of the lawn and seating arrangements under the mulberry trees.

Courtesy Google

We used to pick up this violet fruit and soak it in red wine and found that the result was delicious. One corner of the lawn had a huge barbeque that displayed sizzling and smoking beef, pork, mutton, dumba and chicken spread. The ground floor had a lobby, dining hall tastefully done in Uzbek theme motifs, bead curtain screens and murals. In addition there were special cabins on raised platform with carpets, huge bolsters with lacy screens for partial privacy. A narrow wooden flight of stairs lead to the first floor that housed a huge bar, snookers room and a lounge whereas another flight of similar stairs lead to guest rooms in the second floor. The bar was huge with rough western style seating arrangements spread across the vast room. One cold and wet Friday weekend in the month of January I chose this cabin for lunch with a friend. We started around noon with a bottle of Shiraz Red wine and barbeque snacks. For lunch we ordered a spread of mutton kababs, Uzbek Nan, dumba gravy curry and local leafy vegetables tossed fried in butter along with fresh salad with another bottle of Shiraz. We chatted, ate in leisure, savoring each morsel of food while sipping tasty wine. After finishing lunch at about 4 pm we ventured out and walked around the garden but when it started drizzling we went back to the Mughal cabin and ordered black coffee with Samarkand baked cookies. It was around 6 pm that we felt little cold and ordered another round of coffee and my friend ventured out of the cabin looking for the loo and came back with very fresh bun and homemade butter. We ate that tasty combo with another round of steaming black coffee. Thereafter we lost track of time and space and ordered the third bottle of wine. By now it was around 8 pm and we both felt hungry and ordered dinner of more kababs, salad, and Uzbek bun with butter and gorged on it wholeheartedly. After dinner it was another bottle of Shiraz for the night cap. By the time we finished dinner and emptied the fourth bottle it was 10 pm and high time to leave. This is the first time in our lives that both of us had spent a fantastic ten hours in a restaurant eating lunch, afternoon tea and dinner in one go. It was a record of sort. Amazingly, even after gorging so much of food and wine we were absolutely fit, neither drunk nor overeaten. Cheers to Samarkand.

Uzbek Pulao   King size Naan

(courtesy Google)

I fell in love with the place so much that later on I used to take my other buddies, Praful, Michael and Shyam for after dinner drinks and enjoyed many evenings doing so. We were required to deposit our weapons at the entrance but never did, just walked in with the Beretta under the belt covering it with jacket. I felt it was always unsafe to be weapon free in such places just in case. At the bar I came across US Veterans working for Security Agencies, most of them styled as wanabe Rambo. There was a huge bar and I found some American Ladies working in NGOs used to double up as bar girls. Another evening in Samarkand I came across a tall and shy US veteran and as we started talking about our previous lives in the services, he told me he was a F-16 Pilot who had flown missions over Iraq. All veterans want some years of active service after retirement; it is the same all over the world. It is only when we cross the boundaries of our nation and get into the international arena and mix with people from other countries that we find all human beings are all same, all servicemen are same except for certain exceptions who are psychologically conditioned to think and understand that that one gets a one way ticket to the heaven by killing a non-believer infidels. May God have mercy on their deep rooted, indoctrinated and unshakable belief that has caused so much of violence all over the world. After I returned home I named my little home bar, "Samarkand". There were other international bars and restaurants such as La-Atmosphere, a French pub, Indian restaurants, Dillli Durbar, Anar that served typical Delhi type Indian fare. The UN compound had a well-stocked coffee house that served excellent coffee, baked items and snacks. I can never forget Tony, a Goan manager of UN Canteen who, on my jokingly casual request, organised my favorite dish of baked pomfret in Goan spice. I frequently ate lunch in UN Canteen that served good standard western food at a reasonable price. In another adventure when Praful and I walked in to a Turkish restaurant we were delighted to be welcomed by a very beautiful lady, but utterly disappointed when the lady talked to us in a very hoarse male voice and we realized she was a transgender receptionist cum entertainer.

Risky drive to Bagram:

Once Praful and I took a risky drive from Kabul to Bagram the most important US Army Base in Afghanistan. It was about 70 kms drive that took us about an hour plus. All we had to do was follow road Kolula Pushta inside Kabul and catch Highway 76 that would take us straight to Bagram over a very well paved road built by Americans. The road was generally isolated with few shops scattered along and it was quite possible to be attacked, ambushed, abducted or killed by Taliban. Once we took the decision I depended on my intuition, a 9 mm Beretta pistol with 2 filled magazines and a shot gun with

6 rounds under the car's carpeting. Sometimes I honestly wished that Taliban would approach me because I really wanted to blow couple of Taliban faces into small pieces of flesh and bones. I was and still am angry with them for the merciless killings and torture they inflicted on innocent children, women and men who had done no harm to them or to anybody. The drive in the Hyundai Terracan SUV was smooth and enjoyable. We halted half way in a way side shop and bought some energy drinks to quench our thirst. No dhabas with instant masala tea like India that is what I missed the most. I found almost all Afghans were almost addicted to coke or energy drinks. We reached Bagram Base but as expected it was like an impregnable fort with entry points most cautiously and deliberately guarded. Like all other vehicles we were allowed to enter the first barrier and that was about it. We were politely turned back from the second barrier. I understand it is a massive military cantonment inside the fortress, a world by itself. Notwithstanding such a formidable fortress there have been few bold but unsuccessful attacks on this base. Almost adjacent to the base, Bagram was a small dusty village that had a flourishing market of second hand US Army equipment and clothing. It is a system all over the world that when a military camp is established the area around it starts developing in to a small market that sells much needed local amenities to the soldiers and also acquires and sells handy military surplus or second hand items such as clothing, equipment, blankets, sleeping bags, rucksack, torch lights, knives and second hand goods to the civilians, a parasitic bazar adjacent to a military base.

We looked around this dusty bazar and found that most of the shops were selling second hand or discarded Army Equipment. I bought a Binocular for $ 5, a multipurpose knife with pliers, a miniature Swiss knife with a pencil torch light for $ 2. Also available were Army ration REM (ready to eat meal) packages for $5 per packet that turned out to be quite tasty. Some shops were also selling Viagra Tablets with expired date for $10 per tablet. It is possible to find interesting and useful items in such second hand military stores. We looked around for tea shops but none was available, like Afghans we also bought coke cans and took the highway back to Kabul. It was risky but the adventure was worth the trip.

Bombs and Kalashnikovs, the Kabul Way of Life:

Kabul was a unique place in more than one way. At night we often heard rat-tat-tat of AK-47 assault rifle, sometimes distant and sometimes too close for comfort. All we could do was to sleep with pistol under the pillow and a shot gun next to the bed hoping for the best. Next morning we used to find the walls of nearby houses riddled with bullets. Bomb blasts along the road that specially targeted towards ISAF convoys, Afghan Army and Afghan Police vehicles were frequent occurrences. Every morning our company staffs used to move in four vehicles in a loose convoy letting other vehicles come in between but not losing sight of each other using radios to maintain communication. One such morning as we were crossing the city limits I saw about 100 yards ahead a wheel barrow filled with goods suddenly crossing the road at a speed. There was an Afghan Army bus between my second vehicle and Praful's leading vehicle. What happened next was "Boom", a blast, as suddenly the wheel barrow rammed into the side of the Afghan Army Bus and blew up. There was a huge explosion right in front of me and I could see the debris and splinters flying all over with some falling over my vehicle. My driver, Rafi, rammed the brakes instantly out of driver's reflex and the vehicle came to a screeching halt few feet from the exploded bus. Before further damage and more attack could happen, purely on reflex action I told the driver to reverse full speed which he did but had to brake again to save it from crashing against our own follow up vehicle. I knew from past experiences that in matter of minutes ISAF and Afghan Police patrols would arrive deploy and seal the area. If the attackers have not melted away there would be heavy cross firing and our little convoy would be right in the middle of this cauldron, just like the Harrison Ford movie, "Clear and Present Danger". My concern was for the leading vehicle and Praful, so I called him and was relieved by his instant response. When he said he and the vehicle were ok I told him to drive on and proceed to the company factory without pausing as there could be more attacks. There was a big commotion and the road ahead was blocked. I managed to collect the remaining vehicles and took them back to the guest house. Everyone was shaken up. To defuse the situation and cool the flayed nerves of our staff and drivers I bought a goat in the nearby Kote-Sangi market along some beer cases and organised an instant barbeque in the guest house and told the management that it would have to be a holiday now. This is the pattern we followed as an unwritten Standard Operation Procedure, that is after major blasts or firing attacks we organised a barbeque part to cool the nerves. Equally important aspect after these attacks, besides ensuring the security for property and personnel of the company, was to pacify and cool the frayed nerves of the staff. Impromptu barbeque was the best antidote. Another time there was a rocket attack in the vicinity of our company. The only way to check the attack and damage was to climb the roof of the factory building and observe the area. Luckily the rocket had missed our factory and landed in a nearby field. The rooftop became my observation post during such times. I was not surprised when, after the bomb attack episode on the ANA bus, one of our colleagues took casual leave on compassionate grounds, left Kabul in a hurry and never returned. Another time, Praful, our National Sales Manager was in the market place on his sales work when gun fire broke out and he came under the cross fire. He rang me up and told me that he could see two local men had been shot down and had fallen on the road side. He was in great stress and asked for immediate direction. I told him to get into the vehicle and move away from the spot as fast as possible to any direction permitted by traffic and make as much distance from the incident site". He did that and gave me his location after 20 minutes. I could see that he was closer to our residential area Karte-Se, so I told him to find his way to our guest house and stay there and have a beer. In the evening when I got back we had another barbeque and lots of beer. I found that even the United Nations camps in the city followed this simple procedure. Another time I was in the UN campus enjoying coffee and snacks with a friend. As known the UN Campus was the most protected and fortified place in the conflict zones of the world and Afghanistan was no different. Inside the compound life was secure so that many offices could function in near normal peace condition. There have been instances of vehicle loaded bomb attacks in the UN campus in the city but so far the attackers could only reach and damage the gate barriers. In the middle of our coffee session we heard continued bursts of firing outside the compound. Immediately the UN compound got alerted and as my friend explained the code was red city alert. This meant the gates were sealed and no one could get in or get out. Immediately we had to vacate the coffee house and my friend led me to an underground bunker. To my pleasant surprise I found myself in a huge lounge and a bar. People were already there and more trooping in. Life was so normal; we ordered our drinks, picked up some snacks and headed to a corner lounge and waited out the next 4 hours drinking, chatting and playing billiard. Firing continued outside and normal life continued inside the UN campus. Later we came to know that the firing had taken place between two factions of Taliban mujahedeen. I learnt that almost every house in Afghanistan had some kind of weapon and huge cache of ammunition and it was usual for people to come out of their homes and fire shots in the air to express happiness or anger. Old habits die hard. It was also usual to find landmines along Jalalabad Road. More often than not I used to see a portion of the road barricaded by ISAF troops after detecting mines causing delays and traffic snarls.

Arms Bazaar:

Our company needed weapons for our security staff and on enquiry I found that there was an Arm's Bazaar in Kabul in the area of Zaman Khan Market. Rafi, my driver, took me to a crowded market place near Makriyon and parked the vehicle in designated parking. Thereafter he started walking and I followed him. We walked through crowded lanes and by-lanes of the Zaman Khan market. If I say that I was not worried I would be lying but the sense of adventure in exploring the inner world of Kabul was exciting venture into such places without back up and escorts except for the loaded pistol tucked under my belt. With a mix of Aryan-Mongolian face supporting French beard atop 5 feet something and wearing a base ball cap I could pass off as a local Hazara Afghan. I mostly wore jeans or cargo pant, jacket or sleeveless jackets, baseball cap, Afghani scarf and sporting shades that many people guessed me to be a Turk or Malaysian. It suited me well to merge with the crowd on the street in a place like this where the next person could be an Indian or an anti-Indian Taliban looking to shoot or behead an Indian. My driver led me into a huge market place inside what looked like the ruins of an old fort. We walked through narrow lanes winding through rows and rows of shops selling leather wares, dry fruits, spices, tinned food, biscuits, garments etc. Suddenly, I found myself in a lane that had rows and rows of shops with hundreds of guns of all types. The driver took to a shop he seemed to know the owner, said something in Dari introducing me. The owner took me inside and switched on the lights to reveal a huge cache of weapons of all types. I started checking some guns from the shelves that looked like a western movies gun shop. I was told that 12 bore guns in Afghanistan did not need licence. I sampled couple of gas operated auto loading guns with short barrels that could be used at close quarters as also carried inside a vehicle easily without drawing attention. For test firing the shop keeper gave me special cartridges with a small calibrated detonator that could harmlessly be test fired outside the shop. It was something new and very exciting as I had only seen these kinds of shot guns only in Hollywood action movies. I was told that most of these guns were made in Pakistan, probably in Frontier Province of Baluchistan. I bought 6 guns for 200 USD each and dozen boxes of ammunition. All these were packed nicely in cartons and after payment the owner sent a boy to carry the packet to my car. It was a feeling of warmth, safety and security to have these weapons with us in the company premises. The security managers and supervisors were trained to handle these weapons and test firing was carried out in the nearby firing range of the Afghan Army.

Firing Practice at the Army Firing Range:

Range Firing was another adventure as we had to obtain permission of the Army. I went to the Army Training Centre along the same Jalalabad Road and asked to meet the Commanding Officer by using my nationality and army rank, it worked and the CO was a nice affable guy who received me in his office and offered the same black Afghan tea that I detested.

Range Firing – 12 Bore Shotgun & 9 mm Beretta Pistol

After receiving a written permission from the CO we had to get the range permit from another office that was lorded over by a young sergeant. He looked at the CO's permission letter for a long time as if trying to decipher a secret code. Finally he looked at me and spoke in a halting Urdu and asked me if I had an extra cell phone sim card. I told him that I will arrange one when we come to fire the next day. When I asked him that I wanted target he took me to a store and showed stacks of tin targets and asked for 1 USD per target. When I said ok he quickly picked up a dozen targets and brought it outside. Next day I took the security staff and company directors to the range and organised a competition for shot guns and pistols. I found that Michael, my Phillipino Deputy was a very good shot and he won the pistol shooting where as I bagged the hip firing shot gun shooting. We awarded ourselves with a can of beer each and celebrated the weapon procurement and firing practice with Dumba barbeque that evening downing it with cans and cans of beer.

Graveyard of Russian Tanks

The route to the range was exciting as we crossed rows and rows of destroyed Russian Tanks, the graveyard of Tanks. Later I also bought for the company pistols, AK-47 Rifles and ammunition from a friendly grey market arms dealer. The dealer was a young well educated man who became friend and took me pub crawling in the city's pubs tucked away in nooks and corners. After drinks he would become emotional and discuss his marital discord and divorce plans with me. At risk of abduction and kidnap I visited shady ammunition dealers in remote areas along Jalalabad Road to buy ammunition for the company weapons. Wherever I went to such places I ensured a well-knit back up under my deputy. Besides, a deep gut feeling of safety, not trusting anyone blindly and keeping completely alert with cocked pistol well concealed under the jacket or Afghan scarf helped. There was a good reason to suspect the unknown and be prepared to draw and fire any time. I was lucky and on hind sight as I look back now, even with all the precautions and back up, it was quite foolhardy to take such a risk. *"Fools rush where angels fear to tread".* But then again, no venture no gain, I enjoyed every moment of this adventure that not many, specially at my age, would think of even trying.

Chinese Restaurants

During a Friday weekend, I was driving through Share-Nav with Michael; it was an up market cum residential area which is just outside the main market place. As we drove along, I was attracted by a brightly painted sign board, "Chinese Restaurant". Being a Chinese foodie I *was* thrilled to find one and suggested to Michael that it would be a great idea to step in for Chinese lunch. He smiled and parked the vehicle. We had to walk up a wooden staircase to get to the first floor landing and Michael pressed the doorbell. The big polished door was opened by a middle-aged Chinese lady in a flowery skirt and blouse with full make laced by blood red lipstick and a broad smile to match. She said, "Welcome, welcome" in a heavily Chinese accented English. We stepped into a wide corridor that lead to an open door with heavy pink curtains. The interiors looked neat and polished and loud foot tapping western music wafted through the curtained door. The lady led us in through the curtains and we entered a different world unimaginable in Afghanistan. The hall was reverberating with foot taping loud Western Music, there was a spacious lounge and bar where good looking young and middle-aged Chinese women attired in very modern western skirts, sarongs, maxis and jeans were lounging around in sofas and bar stools. In their company were about half a dozen uniformed American soldiers in their battle fatigue, weapons loosely slung on their shoulders. These soldiers were slow dancing holding their Chinese partners close and tight. Other soldiers were drinking in the bar and sofas in company of Chinese girls and yet some of them were sitting close with and chatting with the girls. Initially I did not register the concept of the place, so when a lady came and asked me, "how can I help you, do you want to go upstairs to the room", I asked for the menu. She smiled and told me in broken English that they did not have menu but food and drinks were available as also nice air conditioned rooms upstairs. I ordered fried rice, hakka noodles and chilly chicken. By then we were seated on the sofa in a corner opposite the bar and I found that Michael was already sitting close and chatting with a beautiful girl. Opened beer cans materialised served by one of the girls in a very tight mini skirt and very low neckline that exhibited most of her upper body assets and I suspected that Michael was behind the liquor order. Suddenly it dawned on me that I was sitting inside a Chinese Whore house with US Army in company. My first reaction was to get the hell out, not because I was averse to the place but because of what my military mind appreciated the place to be a lurking danger. A Chinese whore house in the middle of Kabul with loud Western Music and American Soldiers in battle fatigue and weapons was the best recipe for disaster, a sure Taliban attack. It was de-facto a Chinese bomb about to explode on my face. I nudged Michael and told him, "Let's get the hell out of this place, it is a whore joint and we can be under fire any moment." Michael gave me that smile again and told me, "sir, nothing will happen, just relax, it is a regular place". I was not convinced. In the meantime food came so I decided to eat quickly and get out. I wolfed the food and flushed it down with beer in quick gulps and told Michael to do the same. I asked for and paid the bill and left in a hurry, Michael in tow, albeit most reluctantly. In days that followed Michael used to tell me about his exploits in many such Chinese Restaurants. He told me that the rates were rather cheap with 50 USD for one seating and 100 USD for the whole night. He also used to tell me that the girls were brought on contract from China for a period of time and these "Restaurants" were opened for the benefit of Western expats and soldiers with tacit understanding, if not approval, of the Government. It was a thriving business and everybody seemed to be in win-win situation. Western Armies understand and take such issues as natural biological needs of any man away from home for a prolonged period specially under trying conditions of war zone. They also have a system of R & R (Relief & recreation) where in troops get a week's break every quarter so that they can go out of the battle zone, to family or to another peaceful country nearby, relax, have their biological needs fulfilled and join duty refreshed. UN also follows this system of R&R for its officials and staff. Understanding that biological needs or desires all human beings are same. there is a need to appreciate this human aspect in the modern age in our country and modify leave policy to ensure regular R&R with family or elsewhere. It is indeed a good idea to recognize basic biological human needs and do something about it instead of beating the drum of morality and unable to react when faced with indiscipline connected with such issues. This is why when troops get a chance they go berserk and even cause trouble. This reminds me of an episode in our own Army during the early 70s. A division commanded by legendary General Inder Gill, famous for his forthrightness, had many VD (Venereal Disease) cases amongst soldiers in his division. The then Corps Commander wrote a "Stinker DO (Demi Official)" letter to General asking for his explanation. General Gill replied in a terse, no nonsense, and one sentence letter, "Dear General, I have men in my Division". Matter closed. There is a nationwide need to understand such important human issues in the Asian countries and legalise prostitution in the correct perspective. This will give much needed security, health care and children education to the prostitutes and remove the touts, sex slavery and the connected violence. It may also perhaps check the rampant sexual violence against women.

Social Life

It was interesting to be among a truly multinational melting pot of people from varied background and countries. I was fortunate to roam the streets of Kabul, eat 'Dumba' (Mountain Sheep) meat "Kababs" with Afghan Nan as big as medium size round table. I ate with relish Uzbek Pulao and road side kebabs. I visited local homes and tried to relish tasteless black tea or sugared water melon with coke, strangely a staple diet of Afghans. I befriended Afghans, attended their marriages and birthday parties where we ate food spread on the carpet and women folk never came out in front of the guests. I had a driver called Muhammad Rafi, named by his father after the great Bollywood singer of the same name; unfortunately his father had been beheaded by Taliban for listening to Bollywood music. I came across so many Afghans for whom loosing family members due to bloody killings was a way of life. A tailor in my neighborhood, who I used to patronise, found his small shop gutted by short circuit of electricity and when I helped him reestablish with a $100 donation he kissed my hands in affection and gratefulness and called me brother. However becoming emotional and declaring a guy brother was quite common in that part of the world where as it would be possible for most of them to sell his "brother" to Taliban for few thousand dollars. I was also witness to a meeting in which a Pakistani official threw out couple of Afghans out of the job after declaring that they were blood brothers. I learnt to take this brotherhood business with a huge pinch of rock salt.

I met locals, talked to them, had haircut in local saloons. While doing all the above and many more I carried a loaded 9 mm Beretta Pistol under my belt and concealed by the casual leather jacket. There were blasts and gunfire when we were downtown and there were fear of abduction and I was all ready and waiting to use my pistol to blast anyone trying to harm me or my companions. It is quite unique now to say that most of the Pakistani managers wanted to travel with me in my car for safety. I did not disappoint them showing them a small example on Indian guts. I worked with very nice Greek gentleman who was my boss and a friend till this day, an uneducated and proud Australian who had ego issues with most people. There were Pakistani staff, one of them ex-army. Most of all it was the Indian colleagues who bonded so well to make kind of a family. Praful, a Mallu by birth and an Army brat to boot was the heart and soul of the company and besides being the National Sales manager, was my partner cook and I relished his chilly hot curries and spiced fried ham and sausages.

I found Pakistani managers and staff being superficially friendly but internally suffering from acute inferiority complex and deep rooted jealousy of everything Indian. When I went home to India on leave they asked me to bring them Bollywood movies and Kolhapur Sandals. Some looked genuine enough as they would reply to my friendly "Salaam Wahlekum" with equally friendly "Namaskar". Their religious belief and all things Islam seemed to have been born out of their lifelong indoctrination. Unlike most of us who have knowledge of many religions and philosophies I found them absolutely blank in these matters. In fact all Pakistanis, I came across and had chance to spend some time with, were intellectually bankrupt to the point that they could not think of any subject to discuss except their religion. Of course they would never discuss politics as if the big brother was watching them. In spite of the fact Pakistan was also part of the British Empire; unlike Indians their English Language is poor and written expression almost atrocious. They would be in awe at the effortlessness of Indians in the English language. They respected me but I also found that all of them had very low intellectual level, bound as they were in false sense of religious rightfulness to the extent all religion other than Islam are devil's own. Sometimes, when they would try to discuss the genuineness and rightfulness of Islam, I would quietly tell them that my religion, Hinduism is a way of life and we believe that all religions lead to one God. When I told them that I have read old and New Testament bible and attended every Sunday Church and Temple services in the battalion as also practice Tibetan Buddhism they could not comprehend the idea of such a mixed religion. It was too complex for them. I suspected that most of them thought that I was definitely influenced by the Devil himself. I came across many nationals of Bhutan, Nepal and Bangladesh working in aid projects and the UN. Being a Veteran of Indian Army and of Gorkha origin I was often compared with Nepalese from Nepal when I had to take time to explain the difference between an Indian Gorkha and a Nepali, a national of Nepal.

The First Marathon Race in Afghanistan after 26 Years

As a part of corporate social responsibilities few MNCs and my company decided to organise a public sports programme in the heart of Kabul in Aug 2006. After much deliberations and meetings with the Government officials the event finally chosen was a marathon race for the youth. The idea was to involve the whole city in promoting much needed sports while exhibiting the returning to normalcy in spite of terror attacks and looming threats. Somehow I became an active part of the organising committee that was involved in selection of routes, starting point, finishing points and route logistics. My experience of having been a part of similar event of Army in 1970 in Hyderabad as a young lieutenant came handy. We made a deliberate plan for the event with advertisement, logistic back up, administrative support system and security with police protection along the route, starting and finishing points. There was a huge turnout of runners and Afghans being

123

very curious people there were huge crowd of spectators. The starting point was the famous ruins of Darul-Aman Palace and the finishing point was inside another land mark, the Ghazni Sports Stadium, the killing field of Taliban. It was in this venue that Taliban's Moral Police used to hold public spectacle of quick dispensation of justice to hapless people by flogging and killing them without any mercy. Their spectacles were half burying and stoning to death lovers and women accused of adultery. Perhaps the souls of those wretched and helpless people would still be crying in agony in the same field. Now it was being used for the purpose of sports only. My company sponsored mineral water for the event as also managed the starting and finishing points. Since such a major sports event was being conducted for the first time in 26 years more than half the population of Kabul filled the stadium. It was a great success and win- win situation for all the people of Afghanistan.

Chicken Street & Flea Markets

I strolled around local flea markets and the famous Chicken Street buying knick knacks such as leather jackets made in Turkey, Afghan Shawls and scarves for my family members. It was fun checking out curio shops and road side vendors where it was possible to find some exquisite items. It was here that I found a pair of blue glass candle that matched perfectly with a fruit bowl of the same color and material I had bought from an Afghan in Delhi's "Chor Bazar" (Thief Market) way back in 1995. Incidentally, I was told by both the sellers that items were manufactured in Iraq. Both these pieces still decorate a corner of my drawing room. For quality items of personal use the UN Contractor's Canteen called "Supreme" was the best. It was a chain of Australia based departmental store where everything of human need was available except fire arms. From ice cream, yogurt, chocolates, to frozen meat items, clothes, sports items, beverages to varieties of liquor and wine were available at reasonable price. From the flea market I used to buy dry fruits that Afghanistan is famous for. To keep up with the appetite of international clients there were bakery shops from France & Germany. Once I bought a frozen chicken and when I opened it to cook I found that it was from Brazil. The chicken had flown all the way across Atlantic and travelled through Pakistan to end up on my plate.

Golfing in Dubai

After living in Kabul for a while one carries a kind of mental strain and tension of insecurity without realizing it. Over a prolonged period it could have a telling effect in a psychological level. Once, while having coffee in the UN Coffee shop, a French General told me that whenever he flew out of Kabul Airport he felt relief of a big load of tension leaving his system although he was leading a normal and peaceful life. These are the unknown and unseen factors of such war zones that even if you are out of harm's way and going about your life and job in a normal manner deep down inside one's psyche that lurking danger is playing its part affecting the psyche in an intangible way. It is for such reasons that Western countries have realized the need to get away from work zone to relax, chill out and get back to work refreshed. It was

Dubai at a Glance

in such a context that I decided to take a break and see Dubai.

It was about 2 hour's flight to Sarjah Airport of Dubai. Having got used to the Kabul way of life, its 24X7 security threat any time anywhere, the gloomy atmosphere, dirty roads and poverty, obviously, Dubai was a contrast. It was like landing into the middle of modern day civilization from a medieval war zone. Driving from the airport along the 8 lane super highway to Dubai was like a dream compared to the potholed and dirty roads of Kabul with chances being ambushed and abducted or your vehicle being blown to pieces along with you without much notice. As I checked in to the company guest house in the 47th floor flat of a 5 star hotel I saw the super multistory buildings from the window in amazement. It was indeed a very different world and that reminded me that Kabul, in fact, was the only world of its kind. I visited the super malls, the gold Shuk; the famous gold market mostly owned by Indian Gujarati community and bought a gold and platinum chain for my wife as a Gate Pass upon going home. I visited Marina Beach and saw from a distance the famous ship like structure of Hotel Alburj. However one thing I enjoyed the most in Dubai was a round of Golf with friend Mike, who by then had left Kabul and had settled in Dubai with another job. He picked me up in his BMW and took me to the most beautiful Montgomery Golf Course. It was an amazing experience to play in this world class course specially so after playing in the "World's Most Dangerous Golf Course of Afghanistan". We teed off from No 5 T on a par 5 hole and we both got par, I said "Wow" that was a good start and Nick told me candidly that he thought I was a beginner and had not expected a good standard game from me. He had even brought extra two packets of balls expecting me to loose balls in the course. It was about midday and the temperature in the course was about 50 degree C. Fortunately we were using golf cart driven by Mike. This was my first experience of a world class course as also using golf cart. I found that the cart had GPS system that indicated the flight and distance of the ball. After 4 holes Mike bought us chicken sandwich and coke from the snack shop and we kept munching, and playing. We played 9 holes only as it was too hot to play 18. Mike won but I was satisfied with my 3 pars, 4 bogies and 2 double bogies. Playing in such a beautiful golf course was great pleasure and experience. After the game mike took me to the golf hut that was another piece de art, very tastefully done and the men's locker room was a huge hall with beautiful shower cubicles without doors. Few golfers at this time of the day were moving around naked after shower. We did the same and enjoyed a good shower. Mike dropped me back to the Hotel and left as he had busy day ahead. In the evening I took a cab and went downtown for loaf. I visited Malls and bought a grey striped Pierre Cardin suit with matching light blue shirt and striped tie for 250 USD as also some T-Shirts for golf. I noticed that the Malls had many Indian shops but mostly Phillipino girls as shop keepers. Some Indians and Srilankans were security staff. There was not much to do in the Malls and I got quite bored. I returned back to the hotel and hit the bar for chilled beer and grilled Salmon that was yummy. Refreshed I returned back to Kabul after spending 3 days in Dubai. Flying over Iran was another experience as I watched the reddish desert slipping below me. Back to Kabul to work and more gunfire and bomb blasts to face. As always I felt more comfortable in my own work environment even when it meant Kabul.

Enough is enough-Welcome Home

During stay of a year I flew out of Kabul four times and every time the plane took off from the runway I felt a sense of lightness as if an unseen bundle of heavy weight is suddenly off my shoulder, just like the way the French General had described to me over coffee. Many other expats, almost everyone who worked and lived in Kabul felt the same way. Although we were living a normal life, such as going to work, roaming the city for shopping, playing golf during weekends, going to the restaurants, pubs and hotels like in any other city but deep within us there was a permanent sense of insecurity that we would have to be lucky every day whereas the Taliban or terrorist would have to be lucky only once to get one of us. We knew that it was a possibility; to be attacked, come under cross fire, get blown by land mine or perhaps be abducted by Taliban when we were out in open in the city or on the streets. By the year end whole Afghanistan in general and Kabul in particular was getting increasingly violent with bomb blasts, rocket attacks. Kabul was getting unsafe as days passed. Kabul Serena a five star property of Agha Khan Group was attacked physically by a group of armed men. Intercontinental Hotel was attacked by rocket. Attack on military and police convoys or lone vehicle was regular. Besides there used to be eruption of sudden and sporadic firing in the city with innocent people getting hurt under cross fire. I felt it was time to get out and go back home and not push my luck too far. Enough was enough. I took leave of the company and dear colleague and left for home. On 8th Dec 2006 with great difficulty I managed, through contacts, 3 seats in Ariana flight bound for Delhi as two Indian colleagues were also leaving with me. As the plane taxied and took off towards the Eastern sky to fly over the Hindukush, Pakistan and beyond I felt a great big weight slipping away through my shoulders. Although I was leaving behind a great and unique adventure I was extremely happy to go back home. Thank you Kabul for the great life and adventure you gave me in 2006 and Cheers to Samarkand, I would always miss you! Maybe someday in future I may return just to enjoy a drink with dumba barbeque in Samarkand and enjoy a tour of the Darul Aman Palace restored to its original l glory, just maybe, who knows! Insallah (God Willing), and to quote Arnold Schwarzenegger in the first Terminator movie, "I will be back"!!

Author with Praful & Ramesh in Kabul on 26 Jan 2006

Kalimpong in the 50s & 60s
Life was like that

> *History is lived forward,*
> *We know the end before we consider the beginning,*
> *But we can never really know,*
> *What it was in the beginning!*

> *—Wedgewood, William the Silent*

The Past and the Present

The wheel of time moves slowly but surely, churning events and people across the labyrinth of past, present and future. Ever since the beginning of time, as minutes, hours, days, weeks, months, years and centuries roll on towards infinity, beyond barriers, the past keeps moving further away while getting dimmer and dimmer. Finally a point of time is reached when zillions of events that would have factually occurred in some person's life, alive and kicking at a time and place, would be memories or stories centuries later, albeit in a distorted version. These memories perhaps blink for one last time in the rusty and fading grey cells of the old and infirm before they are finally consigned to the dustbin of life when life itself is extinguished forever. However, chronicles of events recorded in the beginning of known and unknown times have defied the vagaries of change over eons and have lived to tell their tale to a future generation. History is necessary for us to understand our past that shaped our present and for lessons to be learnt from the deeds of our ancestors to chart and correct course towards our future. To quote George Santayana, "Those who cannot learn from history are doomed to repeat it." It is in such a context of unstoppable and ever evolving time and space, that I reflect upon the life and times of my hometown, Kalimpong, from the days in the 50s & 60 when we grew up to the reality of today, a very different world indeed.

Kalimpong in the 50s (Source- Kodak Kalimpong)

Kalimpong today (Source-http://www.yavachitours.com/bhutan/)

Whither Kalimpong

An eagle, flying in lazy circles over the eastern sky around 5000 feet over the hills that cradle the Teesta Valley, looking for prey in the folds of uneven mountainous land below, would see a large spur of ridge line that would look like the saddle of a giant horse fossilized since prehistoric times. Atop the saddle that runs almost east to west, rests one of the most beautiful habitations of the Himalayan foothills. This is Kalimpong, my old hometown. It carries a chequered history connected with Sikkim, Bhutan, Nepal and the British Empire.

From high above the sky, the eagle would see the town sitting rather precariously on the saddle with Deolo Hill as its pommel and Durpin Hill as the cantle. My home town sits at a well balanced and salubrious climatic altitude of 4091 feet and provides a clear view of Mount Kanchenchunga (28,169 feet), the world's third highest peak. River Teesta flows in the valley below, separating Kalimpong hill from Sikkim. The confluence of Teesta and Rangeet below with its small beach of white sand, locally called, *Beni* provides a view of beauty from the southwestern side of the Kalimpong ridge line. *Beni* is the historic venue of a village fair during "*Makar Sankranti*", locally called, *Maghey Sangrati*, the first day of the month of *Magha* that falls around mid January. Kalimpong hill, conjoined with the hills of Darjeeling and Sikkim, is an extension of the foothills of the greater Himalayas that gradually slope down towards the plains of Doors and Siliguri, finally merging with the Gangetic plains of Bengal. Teesta River, sourced in the Teesta Kangse glacial Himalayas in North Sikkim at an altitude of 23189 feet, flows southward through the entire state of Sikkim, mothering numerous streams and rivulets that rumble down the mountains to join her. She is beautiful and placid in azure blue, meandering down the valleys and plains before finally merging with the Brahmaputra River in Bangladesh. However,

Teesta-misty & muddy in monsoon

during the monsoon she is at her muddy best, rumbling down ferociously showing her wrath and causing numerous landslides and devastations along the way.

During the monsoons of 1950 and 1967, Teesta was the mother of all destructions in the hills, even washing away the strong and well-designed bridge near Teesta Bazaar. She flows under the new bridge near this bazaar and rumbles down along NH 31 (Siliguri-Kalimpong/

Sikkim highway) and finally flows under the historic Coronation Bridge before entering the plains at Sevoke about 20 kms north of Siliguri. Approach to Kalimpong from Siliguri (60 kms) is along this NH-31 till Chitrey, 3 km from the bridge near Teesta bazaar, from where NH 31 continues towards Sikkim whereas its offshoot, NH 31A makes a spiral climb of 15 kms to Kalimpong. There is an alternative and less used road for which a traveler has to cross the Coronation Bridge near Sevoke, and drive through Damdim-Gorubathan-Lava along a picturesque landscape, covering a gradual and scenic climb along tea gardens, bamboo groves and pine and rhododendron jungles, a distance of 76 kms in 2 hours. From Lava, the road gradually meanders 31 kms downhill to Kalimpong through mist covered pine and rhododendron forest while touching Pedong and Algarah for a cuppa hot tea or steaming momo.

Confluence of Teesta & Rangeet

Road to Lava

Historically

Over the last 300 years the fate of Kalimpong has been intertwined with that of Sikkim, Bhutan, Nepal and the British Empire as the ownership of this land changed hands almost like the Russian roulette. The simple hill folks of this salubrious foothill have been subjected to a series of turmoil as land passed from one kingdom to another consequent to land grabbing wars waged by ambitious kings of yore.

MotorStand-2014 (Source-Kodak Kalimpong)

Till mid-19th century, Kalimpong area was part of the kingdom of Sikkim but in 1706 Bhutan attacked Sikkim and annexed this area. The ruins of fort, *Damsang Garhi,* built by the Lepchas near Algarah, stands to this day. Sometime in 1780, the Gorkhas of Nepal invaded Sikkim and conquered Kalimpong area along with large areas of Sikkim. After Bhutan's defeat at the hands of the British in 1864, the area was ceded to the British based on the treaty of *Sinchula* in 1865. Around this time, Kalimpong was inhabited by about two or three families of indigenous Lepcha tribe. Between 1866 and 1867, after demarcating the boundaries with Bhutan, the area of Kalimpong and Darjeeling became a permanent part of the British India. The temperate climate of Kalimpong prompted the British to develop it as an alternative hill station to Darjeeling. Encouraged by access to the Nathu La and Jelep La passes along the ancient Silk Route, Kalimpong started developing as an important trading outpost for goods such as furs, wools and food grains between India and Tibet. Such business opportunities attracted migrants from Nepal that led to growth in Nepalese population and their economic prosperity. Later more Nepalese came and engaged in cultivation and dairy farming. As a result of trade Tibetan people also started coming and settled down permanently engaging themselves in business and cottage industries. Since Kalimpong was a part of Bhutan earlier and the trade route to Tibet was through Bhutan it was natural for Bhutanese to be a part of the population. In order to facilitate trade the British Government allotted a plot in 10th Mile area to Bhutan that stands till today as the Administrative and Cultural Center of Bhutan. In the mean time The British masters started coming to Kalimpong, attracted as they were by the temperate climate and beautiful views of the Himalayas. They made themselves comfortable using the abundance of local resources and built cottages and villas and employed the local Lepchas and Nepalese as staff in their work and households.

Mela Ground under the Union Jack-early 1900
(Source-Kodak Kalimpong)

The next obvious step for the British was to spread Christianity. Accordingly, to consolidate their occupation, the British initiated the process of spreading Christianity in the region. The arrival of Scottish missionaries saw the construction of Churches, schools and welfare centers. Around the same time the famous Macfarlane Church was established in the mission compound near the Kalimpong Girl's High School. Rev. W. Macfarlane, a Scottish Missionary in the early 1870s, established the first school in the area. The Scottish University Mission Institution (SUMI) was opened in 1886, followed by the Kalimpong Girls High School. To provide a home for the destitute Anglo Indian children born out of the British masters and the local women, especially those in the mushrooming tea garden areas, Reverend J.A. Graham founded the Dr. Graham's Homes in 1900. Accordingly the Scottish Missionaries started preaching and converting local people into the Christian faith, most of whom were the Lepchas. Consequently, today the entire Lepcha community is Christian. These schools enforced a compulsory period of Bible class every day. By 1907, most schools in Kalimpong started offering education to Indian students and as a result by 1911, population increased to 7,880. Thereafter came the Roman Catholic priests from Switzerland who established St Joseph's Convent, St Augustine's School, St Philomena's school, Churches and dispensary. They also established the famous Swiss Dairy farm in 7th Mile area that made Kalimpong famous for processed cheese and lollypop, and the legacy is present even today. During this period many English people acquired properties and settled down in Kalimpong, building beautiful cottages and gardens.

Dr Graham's Home 1938

Following the Indian independence in 1947, Kalimpong became part of the state of West Bengal. After China's annexation of Tibet in 1959 followed by Indo China war of 1962, many Tibetan families and Buddhist monks fled Tibet and established monasteries in this town. This turn in history led to closure of Jelep-La and Nathu-La passes and the once flourishing trade with Tibet stopped, slowing down the economy. Even after the independence many Britishers chose to remain in Kalimpong and some of them continued to run schools and hospitals they had pioneered. Eventually their population dwindled with the passage of time.

Kalimpong Today

As I look back to the 50s and 60s from the streets and buildings of today, not so faded memories take me back to my own boyish times, the Kalimpong of midnight's children, as our generation was born during the Indian Independence era within the four walls of parents' bedrooms as home deliveries. The simple, peaceful and almost sleepy village town cradled within the raw nature of ever refreshing and beautiful Himalayan foothills has metamorphosed over the last 60-70 years into an overcrowded concrete jungle inhabited by a generation of different species that practice different culture and ethos. The "Y" generation of today, identified by trousers slung so low as to exhibit their colorful underpants with the "Y split" of their posterior, few inches above the anal hole. They sport hairstyles that symbolize a crossbreed between a porcupine's spikes and multi color feathers of a peacock. These gizmo geeks seem to be aimlessly wandering towards nowhere with mobile phones stuck to their cheeks while wire tentacles protruding out of their ears and pockets. Although in groups, each one of them is seen either gazing at their machines on the palms of their strange dragon tattooed hands or talking and smiling to a different world. Walking the same streets today I observe with wonder the sea of humanity, moving hurriedly along the narrow streets clogged by hundreds of carbon emitting vehicles of all sizes and shapes and more vehicles parked using every inch of space making my old home town a de-facto parking lot and a pedestrian's nightmare. The scene is unlike my time in the 50s when only a few people walked on the streets with smiles on their faces and "hello" on their lips for each other whereas the traffic comprised of a few cars, bullock carts and mule caravans. Today I see shops along the roads and lanes bursting with hip hop fancy apparel, electronic gizmos and plastic wares with curtains of synthetic food & tobacco addiction packets that convey a bizarre sense of decoration. Gone also are the old tea shops that sold hot snacks such as, *Singada, Piazee, Nimkee, Bhuja, Dalmooth* with a hot glass of tea, a special delight during winter days. Gone also are the Tibetan & Chinese *momo shops* selling steaming hot pork and beef momos with yummy soup, now mostly replaced by roadside fast food vendors selling tasteless vegetable momos and yellow colored chowmein.

English Cottage of old days still stands today in Dr Graham's Homes

School Boy's Reflections

The early 50s were the end of the British Era and the beginning of independent India. Kalimpong was a laid back and sleepy little village town, the silence punctuated by the musical bells of horses and mules of caravans from Tibet. Those were the days of peace and tranquility; the hills were beautiful, sparsely populated and the word "pollution" was never used. The roads and areas outside town were dotted with beautiful villas, cottages, thatched huts and small buildings, with flowers everywhere, unlike the sea of humanity in the concrete jungle of today. Almost every house had flower gardens with roses, geraniums, chrysanthemums, gladioli, orchids, marigold and anthurium spraying riot of colors from balconies and verandahs. "Glengarry" at 8th Mile had the best rose garden in town, tended by an elderly British couple.

Along the countryside such as *Mongbul Busty, Chuba Busty, Sindeybong Busty, Bong Busty* were green terraced paddy and corn fields, while smoke puffing thatched huts surrounded by colorful flower and vegetable gardens were a perfect balance of tranquility and peace. There was a lingering but pleasant presence of British legacy, as visible with many "white people" still around town especially in missionary schools, hospitals or retirees who lived in their English and Scottish cottages. Who can forget Mr. Scott, the tall Scotsman, Principal of SUMI who freely mixed with, punched and teased his students, Dr Craig, the surgeon of Missions Hospital who saved many a lives, Miss Scrimger, Principal of Girls' High School and Miss Wallace the no nonsense teacher? Today's famous Swiss cheese available in my friend Pran's "Larks", was pioneered by the Swish priests in 7th Mile area during the 40s. It would be almost impossible for the TV, internet, laptop, cell phone and i-pod generation of today to even remotely fathom the ways of the world of Kalimpong of the 50s and 60s. In those days the Main Road used to be almost silent except for the movement of school children during the mornings and late afternoons. On the crowded and congested Main Road of today where Marutis, Hyundais, Santros, Sumos, Boleros Scorpios and screaming motorcycles whiz past every second, we saw few Morris, Austin, Hillman, Land Rovers, Ford and Chevrolet trucks punctuated with bullock carts, horses and mules.

Main Road in 1950 (Source-Kodak Kalimpong)

Main Road in 2014

Books & Classics

Those days we were fortunate to be able to read and understand great classics through illustrated books called Classics colloquially called *comic*. It was easy and enjoyable to read classics like *Hamlet, Ivanhoe, Black Shield, King Arthur, Robin Hood, Jane Eyre, Huckleberry Finn, Treasure Island, Daniel Boon, the Last of the Mohicans* and more. These picture books transported the reader to the scene of action in those historic worlds of heroes. We also got hooked in western comics such as *Buck Jones, Kansas Kid, and Lone Ranger* that gave fair idea of life in the wild west of America. Himalayan Stores that stands erect even today, provided varieties of classics, comics, books and magazines like *Life, Times, National Geographic and Illustrated weekly of India*. They even had Hollywood gossip magazines on their shelves. Kashinath Book Stores below Girl's High School was opened in 1955; however, the oldest bookstore in Kalimpong is *Upasak Brother's Book Depot* mostly selling school text books. All these book institutions stand tall to this day. I also remember reading my first Hindi novel, an action adventure, *Daku Man Singh* during a winter holiday. Another winter I sat over the haystack basking in the winter sun and read the Nepali language *Ramayana* that was like today's high voltage action movie. During another winter holiday I read a Nepali romantic classic *Bhramar*" (Bee) by Rup Narayan Sinha. All these experiences gave me a lifelong reading habit that I enjoy to this day.

Money Value of the 50s

There is an old Gorkha folk song that goes as, ***"Ooiley Bajey ko pala ma, rupeea ganthey dala maa, ailey hamro pala maa makai chainan dala maa"*** (During old days of our forefathers, money used to be counted by baskets but today in our times even corn grains cannot be counted by baskets). When our elders told us that during their days, in the 30s and 40s rice used to cost 1 anna per *sher (equivalent to little more than a kilogram)* we used to laugh. In the same vein it will be hard for today's generation to fathom the prices during the 50s. The monetary system was based on the British system of *rupia, anna and paisa* whereas notes and coins had the stamp and picture of British Monarchs. 16 annas made 1 rupee and 4 *paisa* made 1 *anna*. The coins were mostly made of copper and nickel. Those days with 3 annas we could buy half a glass tea, a plate of *aloodum* and a plate of *Bhujia (namkin mixture) or Nimki and a Singada (samosa) for 2 annas*. In a cold winter day with 4 annas in pocket we would rush to a momo Shop and have a plate of steaming beef momo (4 pieces) with unlimited soup. Pork used to be the all-time favorite at a cost of two rupees fifty annas per *Sher*. Metric system of money was introduced during the mid-50s and it used to be called *naya paise* (new money). So 4 *annas* became 25 paise and 8 *annas* became 50 *paise* whereas 100 *paise* made a *rupee*. Our school fee at SUMI was between Rs 1.50 and Rs 2.00 per month and when we received a stipend of Rs 30 it was a jackpot. It would also be interesting to note for today's generation that paying guest rate was a standard Rs 30 per month whether one stayed in someone's house or ate at a hotel on a monthly basis. Even in 1960 when I was in class X and used to eat at *Karim Hotel* near *old Novelty Cinema hall* and later at *Narbada hotel in Thana Dara* (Police Hill) it was Rs 30 per month. A cinema ticket at the lowest class was 5 annas that scaled up to 10 annas for mid-level and 12 annas for the last few rows whereas balcony used to cost Rs 1 and 4 annas and dress circle Rs 2 and 8 Annas. Petrol cost Rs 2 per liter so with enough pocket money once in a while, I would approach a friendly driver at the motor stand, buy one liter of petrol and request him to teach me driving. This exercise would take me on a driving lesson to Durpin Hill and back with friends tagging along. My eldest sister's teacher's salary in Mission's Girls High School was Rs 50 per month in 1950 that rose to Rs 75 by 1958. A fashionable handmade pair of boots with white crepe sole used to cost Rs 30 and vegetable for one week could be bought for Rs 20.

Bicycles and Motorbikes

During those days we could see just one or two bicycles in town; one was owned by an elderly Chinese gentleman from 7th Mile who pushed it to his work place, the Industrial School, every morning and glided back home after work. My friend Dhurba Pradhan tells me that he and his friends always helped the Chinaman push the bicycle uphill while on way to school. Mass bicycles were brought to Kalimpong sometimes in 1956-57 by Tshering Bassi of 10th Mile and hire charges were expensive, Rs 2 per hour. Most of my generation learnt cycling during this time in Mission Ground located below McFarlane Church. Saturdays, after the school it was cycling to 8th or 14th Mile and back, a great thrill of speed for the young boys. As regards motorcycles, called, *bhatbhattey* after the noisy *phat-phat* sound they made one such machine was owned by the priests of St Augustine's and the second three wheeled motorcycle, either Matchless or Indian Chief was owned by Joe of St Augustine's. Once I saw him carry the entire hockey team of his school on his bike across town to Dr Graham's Homes.

Road building in the 50s (source-Kodak Kalimpong)

The Radio: Besides the occasional movies at *Kanchan* and *Novelty* Cinema Halls another source of entertainment was the radio. It was common to hear Hindi Film songs blaring from radios of *paan* shops lining the Main Road. As we walked to school every morning, songs could be heard almost continuously on popular Radio Ceylon morning Programme and sometime we heard Nehru's speeches. I remember during the Chinese aggression war of

1962 the whole town listened to the 8 am news in a tense and grim mood. On the lighter side who can forget the *Binaca Geetmala* presented by Ameen Saini as popular songs blared from the radios every Wednesday. Young men on the street and drivers at the motor stand would join in the chorus. Motor stand was a place to hear the live performances by drivers and cleaners in gay abundance. Radio brands were HMV, Murphy, Phillips and some homes had radiograms that could play 8 LPs (Long Playing Records) one after another, a great possession those days.

Saturday the Special

Since time immemorial Saturdays have always been very special in Kalimpong, more than a holiday- a festive, enjoyable, relaxed and fun filled day that only people of Kalimpong can experience and I am so happy to see that this culture continues today. It is something along the lines of what today's metro people would call TGIF (Thank God It's Friday) mood. Our school had only games for 2 hours till 11 am- holiday thereafter. Games in school was always fun, be it football in Mission ground or Carmichael ground or volleyball in the school ground. The school team practiced on the best court and the rest were occupied on the first come first serve basis. Our gang leader, Himananda Khati was always there with a new ball and the net standing at the center of the court till all the gang members reached. "RESERVED" was the signal for the rest. After the school our programme was visiting Saturday *Haat* (market day) in the morning and eating snacks in the open stalls, watching football matches in the afternoon with matinee shows at *Novelty and Kanchan* cinema halls squeezed in between. As against net romance, net dating and net marriages of today, Saturdays were the only days for dating for the romantic teenagers. Kalimpong Park, Durpin Hill or Delo Hill were the lovers' rendezvous. The day's romance used to finally culminate in watching a movie where holding hands carefully and occasionally, was the ultimate romantic goal. For shy singles like me a cowboy movie of James Dean, Gregory Peck, Rock Hudson, John Wayne, Tony Curtis or war movie of Audi Murphy was the ultimate finale. Needless to admit now that Hollywood movie was my idea of romance albeit in a visualized form.

The Gang

We had a gang of good students led by the tough, adventurous and talented leader, Himananda Khati (nicknamed Himal) who was very protective towards the gang members and quick to pick street fights when the gang was threatened. He was and still is *mama* (maternal uncle) to all of us since he is my mother's cousin. Some Saturdays, after the school games we planned special operation of raiding fruit orchards of plums and peaches from the big bungalow gardens of Durpin Hill. The strategy was; Himal the leader, would walk to the bungalow most confidently and start a conversation with the caretaker and the rest of us would move stealthily towards the fruit trees and fill up our bags. Thereafter we moved to a prearranged place and call Himal by a whistle signal and enjoyed a sumptuous fruit picnic at a special spot overlooking the town amidst jokes and laughter at each other's expense. It was pure fun and vitamin.

Football Mania

Football was the ultimate game of Kalimpong. It was a game of the entire town and villages nearby. Almost like the *Ramayana and Mahabharata* TV serials of 80s all over India, this footer game captured the attention of the people of Kalimpong with Mela Ground as the main arena. There were star teams like SUMI, Himalayan Sporting, Friend's Union, St Augustine's School, Dr Graham's Homes, and Kumudini Homes.

FRIEND'S UNION CLUB XI
Winners- SATAL SINGH MEMORIAL SHIELD 13[th]JULY 1957
Kalimpong

Standing-(L.to.R) Tsering P. N.Tsering. Badrudin. L.B.Basnet. D.M.Subba.
Sitting-(L.to.R) K.B.Pradhan. Palden Lama. G.Gyalpo(CAPTAIN).L.Dafang.
Ground-(L.to.R) I.S.Subba.   J.B.Darnal.

(Source-Kodak Kalimpong)

There were famous and almost revered football stars who were like celebrities of sorts as they walked the streets. The most famous tournament was Independence Day Shield the final of which culminated on the 15th August every year. The crescendo of crowd frenzy, expectations, tensions, cheering and street fights would keep escalating as the teams moved from initial knock outs, quarter finals, semifinals to the grand finale. During the final match the grassy gallery slopes of Mela ground, all nearby building windows and terraces as also the top of every available truck and bus lining the motor stand used to be filled with enthusiastic spectators like ants on honey. I am glad this and many traditions of the old days carry on even today albeit over a larger canvas.

Special Day-15th August

Kalimpong, perhaps, is the only place in the India where 15th August is one of the most celebrated events with a very different connotation. Most of the festivals are religion or culture based but 15th August is the festival for one and all. In more than one way it even surpasses the main local festivals, Dusshera, Diwali or Christmas. It is a mystery as to how this day became so very special in the life of Kalimpong as this culture has been in practice since times immemorial. The scale of grandeur has only been increasing as the years roll on. What used to be simple celebrations of schools March pasts, sweet distribution, special documentary screening and the Independence Day Football final match in the 50s, has now snowballed into a high voltage celebrations packed with multiple events that are showcased over days. Programmes such as ethnic cultural shows, song and dance variety entertainments, debates, quiz contests; band displays and series of football tournaments are choreographed and stage-managed involving the entire town and neighboring areas. Procuring new clothes just like it is done during Dusshera, Diwali or Christmas is the norm in every household. Out of station residents take leave to be home for this special day. People from the surrounding villages as also from the villages of nearby Sikkim congregate to be part of the celebrations. The day's celebrations are followed by dinner parties at offices, hotels, restaurants, homes and amongst friends while local and foreign liquor flowing in abundance and gourmet bill of fare materialize on the table in every home. The celebrations continue even on 16th August with school's song and dance programme and other events. It is needless to add that the day after the mega event it is two days holiday for all the schools so as to stagger back and find one's feet after the blast. The centre of all celebrations is the legendary arena, *Mela Ground* that has witnessed the hoisting of the Union Jack, the speech of Pt Nehru, football matches including ones played by the late prime minister of Bhutan, Mr. Jigmi Dorjee, all important sports events and avoidable political speeches since times of yore. Most of all it is the mood of the people that is loaded with excitement in anticipation, months before the D Day that culminates into full blast mega mania on the 15th August.

Brawls

Just as today's youth play local cricket on the street, lanes and by lanes, our generation used to play football on narrow roads, gullies, lanes and in villages in court yards and dry paddy fields after harvest. Initially it was a new ball was bought after collecting money. After days of play, when the ball used to be old and torn, we would fill up the case with clothes, tie it up with ropes and get on with the game. Once even this ball turned into shreds we used to play with *Shankhatra*, a large, almost football size citrus fruit, that grew in abundance. Friend Dhurba tell me about street football between rival gangs of 6th and 7th Mile. The game used to be so ferocious and rough that players packed stones, nails and broken bottle pieces over their feet covered with bandage to hurt the players of rival gangs. Sometimes such games degenerated into deadly street brawls with daggers and knives. Similar gangs operated in the lanes and by lanes of town, 10th Mile & Tirpai Hills and fights even reached the schools and class rooms. While in Class VII in SUMI a major fight broke out between two gang boys from town. One was *Doldl* (that was his name) and the other was *Tejay*. Arguments lead to pushing and punching but suddenly *Doldol* had a knife in his hand and Tejay took out his studded belt and crouched menacingly on top of the desks. Only when someone cautioned them about a teacher's approach, did the fight freeze but continued after school hours.

Skating Boards

The famous adage, ""Necessity is the Mother of Invention" was true and practiced by us in our daily play lives. In the villages we would make a contraption of three wheeled bikes with wooden wheels, a flat plank to sit on and a steering of forked branch attached to single wheel. Test tracks used to be slopes in the fields and footpath, where we hurtled down, mostly crashing and hurting ourselves. Boys living near the roads made innovative skating board by fixing vehicle ball bearings on wooden shaft fitted under a flat wooden board, two wheels at the rear and one in the front attached to a steering handle. It worked well and I remember seeing these boys rolling down the main road, screaming, laughing, falling and doing it again and again. Dhurba and his gang from 6th Mile used to pull the skates up the road to 9th Mile Engine Hill and roll down all the way to their area. They were bold enough to take skating boards to town, hide the machines under the bush and go for the late night movies at Novelty Hall. In absence of enough money, they would bribe the gate keeper with some coins. He would allow them to sit on the floor or occupy vacant seats and enjoy the movie. After the show they would pick up their skate boards and roll down the National Highway in the middle of the night with or without fluctuating dim street lights powered by a diesel generator installed earlier by the British administration. Brakes used to be their bare feet screeching against the tarmac road. Later to cope with water shortage, during summer, these skate boards were modified, made bigger and sustainable so as to carry water in huge tin cans. Some innovative boys even used them as small business enterprise for water delivery during the dry summer seasons.

Fashion

The source of fashion in Kalimpong has always been Hindi and English movies. For the boys it used to be drain pipe trousers and loose shirts pulled out loose a wee bit from the waist. We also wore studded and big buckled belts copied from the western movies as also pointed shoes or boots. Most of us copied hair styles of Hollywood stars like Tony Curtis, James Dean & Rock Hudson; sides flattened by Palmolive Vaseline and the top puffed up towards the forehead. Of course there were boys copying Devanand's hairstyle of side parting and wavy top. The most sought after clothes for young boys were blue jeans, checked shirts, leather jackets and cowboy boots, not always available and affordable. However, anyone with connection to people returning from Hon Kong or Malaya could manage such luxuries at a cost. Young girls wore mostly knee length frocks where kurta pajama was just about entering the town as a result of fashion in Hindi movies. My sisters used *Afghan snow* cream and nail polish was called by brand name, *cutex*. *Palmolive hair Vaseline, hawain slippers* had started coming to the market. For the educated office going older men and school teachers the English fashion of 30 and 40s such as 3 piece suits, tie, felt hat, umbrella or walking stick was still in vogue. Conservative elderly men wore traditional Gorkha dress *Daura-Sural* or just *Sural* with shirt and coat. For ladies it was always the *sari* but those in the villages used to sport traditional Gorkha *Goonew* (wrap around) *Cholo* (full sleeve blouse with strings at the front) and *Mujetro* (shawl). At that time it was beyond our imagination to foresee the fashion of the 70s ushered in by the Beatles, the fashion of shoulder length hair, bell bottom trousers and skin tight shirts with large pointed collars.

English Fashion of the 30s & 40s continued in the 50s

Music & Drama

The General public's ear for music was mostly affected by Hindi movie songs of those days with the medium being radio and gramophone records. These songs were played over loud speakers during marriages and functions and everybody used to enjoy the rhythm. At the same time there was a deep love for ethnic and modern Nepali songs. Cultural functions were primarily based on Nepali music and dance of various genres such as modern, folk etc. There were renowned musicians, singers and composers who enthralled the audience with their talent. All the cultural & School function were based on such Nepali music and I do not remember Hindi movie songs being sung at such functions. Even the plays were based on Nepali on the works of Nepali poets and writers. I do remember *Muna-Madan*, a play based on a tragic love story written by a famous Nepali writer, Lakshmi Prasad Deokota being enacted in Town Hall by the Girls' High School students. Legendary singers of those days were *Dilmaya Khati, Tara Devi, Aruna Lama, Shanti Thatal, Amber Gurung, Amar Thapa, Narayan Gopal and Gopal Yonzon* who sang soulful melodies of love, romance and tragedy enchanting the entire hills. Later in the 60s came modern popular songs that were catchy and peppy for those times. Song such as *Swarnim Sapana* (Golden Dream) sung by Ravi

Das became overnight sensation in the early 60s and for a long time it was in everybody's lips. During marriages and religious ceremonies melodious Hindi and Nepali songs were played through loud speakers for several days for the listening pleasure of one and all. It was only during such occasions that we got to hear such melodies continuously for days, mostly during winter holidays. In schools, boys and girls took great interest in music, art and culture. Local school talents performed popular songs during school functions with accompaniment of a small band composed of harmonium, tabla (twin drum), guitar, and banjo. The base guitar sound was produced by an innovative instrument made of a plywood tea chest with a chord strung across on a bamboo stick that could bend to produce high and low bass notes.

Tibetan Connection

One of the striking memories of those young days is the Tibetan mule caravans decorated with colorful regalia and musical bells around their necks, driven by Tibetan men in their traditional *Bacchus* (gown like Tibetan Dress) with prayer wheels in their hands and *OM MANI PEME HOM* on their lips. The mule train was guarded by small but ferocious Tibetan dogs with bells on their collars, however, as I recollect, those dogs were only minding the mules and never did they threaten or even bark at people passing by. During winter months these mule and horse caravan camps filled almost all the empty spaces along the road side,   dotted with colorful Tibetan tents, women going about their chores and children running around or playing with dogs.

Along the old silk route Caravan with wool from Tibet -the early 50s
(Source- Kodak Kalimpong)

The caravans brought wool, carpets, Tibetan and Chinese silk and brocades and took back salt, sugar, spice oil etc. It was a flourishing trade; consequently, part of Kalimpong, 10th Mile onwards, was almost a mini Tibet. Remnants of those trade days still exist in those areas. Today's generation of those industrious Tibetans still practice similar business albeit in the form of cottage industry. They make incense sticks, Tibetan dress, shoes, noodles, china grass and Tibetan artifacts such as wooden dragons, statuettes, prayer beads and many more. However, over the years many hands have changed and major part of the whole sale trade on all Tibetan items are in the hands of the most affluent business class of the hills, *Marwari* who hail from Rajasthan but own major share of business of the hills today. Descendents of early Tibetan settlers have completely adapted to the local culture and ethos and have been doing well for themselves in all walks of life. Besides the business, this community has produced military, police and civil services officers, academicians, musicians, air hostesses. There are many instances of intermarriages with Nepalese, Lepchas as also with other Indians and foreigners. This is process of evolution of mankind.

Wool godown Kalimpong 1887 (Source–Kodak Kalimpong)

Daggers & Legends

Just like in the rest of the hills, people of Kalimpong also refer to distances by kilometers and places by Miles and 10th Mile was the most dangerous area in town with ferocious *Khamba* and *Amdo* Tibetan tribesmen roaming the street armed with *Patang* (sword) and *Chuppi* (Dagger) sheathed in silver scabbard across *kamarbandhs*. Cases of midnight brawls, stabbing and sometimes even killings prevailed. The next morning, school used to be full of stories about such brawls. Besides these Tibetan adventurers there were local goons who were legends of sorts. There was this famous, fearsome but very smart and handsome *Samdoo* who was in and out of Kalimpong jail for brawls and escapades. However, out of the jail into the football field he was a hero to watch. There was *Achu Namgyal* who was a great goal keeper of SUMI in the early 50s, but in another such brawl when he tried to guard himself with bare hands against *Patang* and *Chuppi* attacks his hands were permanently damaged. Such was his spirit that after the wounds were healed, *Achu Namgyal* returned back to the football field, this time around as a full back and he played the game as the most dependable full back, no forward player could get past him. The story goes that he used his damaged hands to pull down the shorts of the forward attackers, just like Maradona's "Little hand of God". Another one was the famous football umpire, *Lamsingh*, whose no nonsense umpiring style and on field antics would put today's international umpires to shame. Such was his style, strictness and amazingly quick gestures to show faults, matched with the rapid whistle blowing, that when he was the umpire, fair play was assured, much to the relief of players and public. Another player, *Purke (Shorty) Jangey* of SUMI played bare feet and scored the winning goal with a high lob from the corner line in the 11th hour of the tense 15th August final match against a tough team, Friend's Union. Another SUMI player, *Mote (Fatty) Jangey*, shot every penalty kick through the net that even the best goalie would not dare and try stop the ball. Not forgetting the legendary, *Shivrattan Periwal* of SUMI and *Bhanu Pradhan* of Kumudini Homes who were famous for stopping most of the penalty kicks at the overwhelming applause of the cheering crowd. Who can forget the high kicks of Gyappan sir of Kumudini Homes-the ball flew across the ground beyond the Motor Stand. There were so many legendary players and heroes but one last mention has to be made of *Pemba, the Keera Kancha*. He was a young Tibetan boy who started as a loom operator at the Industrial School, but an extremely keen player of football that he was nicknamed *Keera Kancha* meaning "football worm". With his multi talents of football, music and humor he progressed very well and retired as games teacher of Government High School. Unfortunately he is no more. RIP Pemba the *Keera Kancha*.

The Melting Pot of People

Initially a part of Sikkim, snatched by Bhutan and Nepal and finally grabbed by the British, Kalimpong became an integral part of Republic of India after the Independence in 1947. As a result of proximity, this little town suddenly became a small sub division of Darjeeling district in the state of West Bengal. So the master of its fate became hitherto unknown Bengal with its state capital in Calcutta now Kolkata. As much as the presence of original Lepchas and inflow of Tibetans, Bhutanese and Nepalese before and after British occupation, presence of small community of Chinese in Kalimpong have an interesting history. Since the eighteenth century the Chinese Government had maintained representatives in Lhasa, known as Ambans as a symbol of Chinese authority in Tibet. However, after the fall of the Qing dynasty (1644-1912) the Amban and his military escort were expelled from Lhasa. Although majority of this group returned to China, a small number, specially those residing in southern part of Tibet in the areas of Yatung and Chumbi valley found it easier to move southwards towards Sikkim and the Darjeeling-Kalimpong hills. They made their living by virtue of their inherent talents and crafts and established small business. This explains the presence of Chinese shoe makers, dentists, and restaurant owners in Kalimpong. I also remember holding my father's hand and watching circus and magic shows performed by Chinese experts in the late 40s and early 50s.

As Kalimpong started growing, it's administrative and logistics needs brought people from the nearby plains of Bihar and Bengal. By virtue of their basic characteristics, people of different regions practiced their trade and services for each other. Marwari's established trade; Biharies provided small but essential services such as tea shops, general merchants, paan shops and cobbler's shops around the streets and street corners. Bihari Muslims established bakeries, Bengalese were brought by the Britishers as clerks and office bearers and later in the banks and railways where as some of them came as teachers. Later they brought their famous Bengali sweets shops. Today the old sweet shop of *Pravash* near the Motor Stand is doing roaring business As a result of the ongoing growth, Kalimpong became a melting pot of people from different nations and regions of India, living in harmony, supporting each other and their children studying in Missionary schools and being friends. It was easy to see this conglomeration of people in a football team comprising of Nepalese, Tibetans, Chinese, Bhutanese, Marwari and a Bihari. Later Thai students joined the fray as good footballers and boxers.

The Royals and Nobles of Bhutan and Sikkim used to be seen galloping around on horses with their beautiful companions or driving around their imported cars. They were often seen in cinema halls, football fields and landmark joints such as *the Gumpus restaurant,* Sanghai restaurant and the *Himalayan Hotel.* The famous film star of yesteryears, Devika Rani Roeirch had settled down in Kalimpong with her Russian painter husband but they were more of reclusive. One fine day Kalimpong was playing host to Prince and Princes of a faraway land, Afghanistan. We saw a group a very stately, dignified and beautiful looking ladies and gentlemen walking around Kalimpong in the Durpin Hill areas. We were told that they had been sent to Kalimpong in exile from Afghanistan. Little did I realize that I would be living and working in their ravaged land after almost 50 years and would visit their magnificent palace, "Darul Aman" (abode of God) razed to the ground by 35 years of war. There was *Vikkshu Sangharakshita,* an English monk who lived alone at his 9th Mile cottage, *Hermitage* residence and patronized local boys, helping them, in studies, teaching English language etc. He also ran a hostel of sorts where I stayed for a year and learnt English through him.

Life in General

Life was lots of walking as everybody walked everywhere. The concept of the local taxi was almost unheard of. Everybody was doing some work as we did not see jobless people wandering about. Ours was pure organic life in today's jargon as most of the meals came from our own fields and vegetables, cottage cheese, butter, curd, cheese available in the market were from local farms. Only the essential oil, sugar, salt, pulses came from the plains. We found great joy in small things of life like playing street football, riding a bicycle, jumping behind a bullock cart, stealing fruits from others orchards, picnicking, having tea and *Singada,* a steaming plate of beef or pork Momo or eating ice cream for the first time. *Mukund Sharma* gave the first Ice-cream shop to Kalimpong during the early 50s. We wore handmade shoes by Chinese shoemakers and ate bakery items from *mobile human bakery* in a large tin box carried on the turbaned heads of *biscuit wallas* who sold their stuff to us kids on credit. Interestingly these mobile bakeries also carried and delivered love letters. The only political parties known were Congress and Gorkha-League but people did not care about politics. Gorkha League, with red & green flag and crossed *Khukuri,* used to sweep the polls and the famous slogan was, *Gorkhas, Bhutias and Lepchas are one.* Compare that with today's *divide and rule politics.* Occasional tourists used to be the camera wielding *foreigners,* perhaps on nostalgic trip to Kalimpong.

Almost every house in the villages maintained flower and vegetable gardens and we grew up on rice, corn, vegetables from own land, milk from own cows, eggs and chicken from home poultry and occasionally pork and mutton slaughtered at home or at a neighbor's house. We ate oranges, pears, figs and bananas climbing and plucking from the trees, played high jump, long jump and pole vault in our terraced fields, swam in the little ponds of clean and not so clean streams flowing by our land, we went to the jungle on picnic, cooked and ate simple rice, *daal,* vegetable and country chicken, obviously broiler chicken was not even born those days. Before cooking time my sisters made us run to the vegetable garden to get tomatoes, green chilies or coriander leaves fresh from the garden that is now termed organic living. My brother Bejoy and I dug and made a small pond in our land and kept small fish and shrimps, caught by us in the streams. It became tourist attraction for the visiting relatives from town.

I did my entire schooling under kerosene lamps and did not feel any discomfort. Sometimes the glass cover would break and had to rush with 4 Annas in hand to a shop by the roadside to get one. As a boy my elder brother and I ran and jumped every movement. We made swords and daggers out of bamboo and played knights read in the classic books. Those days there were no Coke & Pepsi, no mineral water, no TV, no iPods and we grew up outdoors climbing rocks, playing football on the streets and fields and enjoyed harvesting as family picnic. We played hide and seek in and around haystacks and bamboo groves. Today, when I see kids glued the TV, playing computer games, plugged in to the musical net through iPod, I feel sorry for them as they are missing out on so much of the real world; they know only the "virtual" world. Most of them have not seen fruit on a tree or plucked vegetables from a kitchen garden. I wonder where Kalimpong would be in another 50 years' time, same place but different people and very advanced technology and very little of the natural and real world, I wonder if our trees, rocks, school buildings and land would exist at all. I am convinced that mine was a blessed generation, blessed to have been brought up on a simple life of pure organic diet and fresh oxygen.

First Love Affair (One Sided)

She was at the center of a giggling group of girls, an epitome of grace and beauty with an infectious smile. She was fair of medium height, shoulder length hair, cute fringe on her forehead, flushed cheeks, pug nose and round but slightly narrow eyes, a perfect oriental version of Audrey Hepburn. I was mesmerized and could not take my eyes off her. It was 1961. I was a big boy of class X in Government High School and Roman holiday was a Hollywood movie starring Gregory Peck and Audrey Hepburn. That was it; I fell in love for the first time in my life, with Audrey Hepburn. So enamored was I by her beauty that I started searching for magazines with her photos and kept her cutouts in the pages of books. One fine day, when I was walking towards town I saw a group of girls walking down the road from opposite direction. Lo and behold, she was there, im the middle of a group of giggling girls. Thereafter she lived in my head and I started walking the same road the same time of every morning to have a glimpse of her. I confided my discovery and losing my heart to my close friend, Kunzang. He told me that he knew her and obviously I forced him for an introduction. Next day I found myself standing at her doorstep along with friend Kunzang and he knocked. I waited with bated breath. The door opened and she was there smiling at Kunzang. She looked lovely and I was speechless. Kunzang cooked up some pretext, casually chatted with her and introduced me. She looked up with a faint smile at me or so I thought and I froze, Tongue tied, speechless and completely in sweet shock at being face to face with her, at touching distance. That was it. We left her place and I took Kunzang to *Dipali* tea shop for a treat. Over tea and snacks he suggested I write a love letter that he would hand over to her. Great idea. Back in the room, I wrote and re-wrote my first love letter of at least 3 pages till mid-night. Read over it again and again, correcting and editing and finally sealed it with a prayer and a kiss. Next day I gave my most prized possession of my life to Kunzang and waited for the reply with bated breath. Several days passed and my anxiety rose by the day. Couple of days later Kunzang told me that he had delivered and thank God she had accepted it, great positive sign indeed, first hurdle crossed. I waited for the reply, day after day, week after week and months passed. Nothing happened.

I got busy with exams and stopped taking the walk to see her. A Couple of months passed I lost interest and had almost forgotten about Audrey Hepburn. In the mean time I had made friends with a Tibetan Muslim guy called Faiz who was a migrant from Tibet and we conversed in Hindi. One day we went for a movie at Kanchan Cinema Hall and after the movie he told me, "Come this way I will show you something". I said ok and we started walking along the DS Road towards Motor Stand. He told me to look inside a Dry Cleaner's shop as we passed. I was anxious wondering who it was he wanted me to see. As we reached just opposite the dry cleaner's shop, he nudged me and I looked inside. Oh my God, it was her, no other than my very own Audrey Hepburn, sitting inside as beautiful as ever, the same lovely face, the same fringe of hair and the same beautiful eyes. She was also looking in our direction but her eyes looked at Faiz, not me. I was shattered into small pieces right there but my legs dragged me ahead. That was the last time I ever saw her. That was my first, and highly one sided love story. Life moved on and many walked in and out of heart , but Audrey was Audrey, she will always be the epitome of sweet oriental beauty and a printed tattoo of her beauty will always reside in my heart forever. A thing of beauty is a joy forever. No regrets, whatever happens are always for the best, Amen.

Final Year 1962, Government High School (author-Sitting extreme right)

Charting the map of Life

In 1958, upon completing class VIII, the old Matric system changed to new Secondary Education system. This meant higher secondary board final examination in class XI as against the Matric Exam in class X and three streams of Arts, Science and Commerce branched off from class XI onwards. Since my school, SUMI, had only Arts stream at that time, I along with *Suren* and *Homenath* decided to join Kumudini Homes in Class XI science but ultimately we chose to join Government High School for class X & XI.

That is where we set our dreams and started working on it seriously as also made friends with studious fellow students like Kunzang, Sushant and Ajit. Although I had joined Bio Science to become a doctor but after serious discussion with my brother in law, then Major Shishupal Ranpal I decided to be a military officer like him. It is truly said that if we wish to achieve something in life, all we have to do is set the aim and start walking towards it, we will ultimately reach there. We did. Although we had our fun and games as teen age boys do, at the same time, seriousness had set in about making a good future life and the immediate need to get good grades in the final board examination. For that reason we studied as much as we played and roamed around.

1962 was a very busy year in class XI, getting serious for the board exams, Gang wars and fun were over. My father was in Kurseong and all elder brothers and sisters had moved out of Kalimpong for studies and work. My immediate elder brother, Bejoy was in SUMI Hostel and we used to meet once a while. He took care of me so well that when I was down with mums he came to pick me up in a taxi and got me admitted to Mission's Hospital, thereafter he was by my bedside every day with finest bakery items of town. I have no idea how he managed but he even bought me a suit for the Dusshera festival. My eldest brother, Hemant had finished college and was teaching in Pedong and it is he who was financing my education with his meager salary of Rs 75. Rs 30 to me, Rs 30 for his PG fees and remaining Rs 15 for the month. Even with that he would sometimes make it to Kalimpong to see me and Bejoy and give us few annas for pocket money.

I had no place to stay as I did not like the idea of being a PG. It was very kind and gracious of our dear Headmaster, Late Shri KB Gurung who permitted me to stay in a vacant room in the extended part of the school. It was a blessing in disguise as I could study as well as play table tennis and exercise in the parallel bar just outside the room. God always guides and prepares one for the next thing to happen in our lives. I was to join the Army the very next year and this physical fitness regimen helped me tremendously. God is great, he gives you what you need not what you want. Kalzang Bhutia, from Sikkim a good footballer of SUMI, joined our School in class X and became my roommate. Although junior in class he was much older than me and started bossing around, however, being weak in studies, specially in math, he sought tuition from me but when I gave him sums and English readings he would complain of headache and go to sleep. In fact I had three sets of friends, first was my studious gang of Sushant, Ajit, Suren and Shyamal, second was senior guys and football stars and third, the one most close to me was one and only Kunzang. I had already made up my mind to wear military uniform with badges of rank of a captain in the not so distant future. So in spite of doing things that most of the boys do I was very serious for future as such studies was priority. Once, Suren and I got quite drunk with local beer, "Chhang" in a Tibetan home bar. We staggered back to my room and hit upon an idea of testing our brains after drinking. I took out the Trigonometry book and we started doing sums one after other and by early morning we had finished the whole book. Our concept of life was to have lots of fun, lots of experiment but keep the aim straight, have to be something in life, a man of substance. That was the year 1962, the year of the Chinese aggression during the months of September-October. The mood of Kalimpong had changed with the war. So many soldiers from Kalimpong and surrounding hills had died. Whole town was listening to the somber news of war, glued to the radios in the shops. Nation had declared emergency and many youths started joining the armed forces on emergency recruitment. The next year I was to be a part of this process.

Goodbye Kalimpong, Hello World

I finished school as I wrote my final higher secondary board examination in March 1963. After exams I hung around Kalimpong for a week enjoying the end of school nostalgia and last few fun filled days with Kunzang and few other friends. In our time, there were no final year students' farewell or parties and gifts. We finished exams, had fun with close friends and moved on. After my last one week in Kalimpong mostly with Kunzang, I left for Kurseong where my father and youngest of the sisters, had made home. Fortunately my sister, Rukmani was working in the local Railways Office and was very supportive to my ambition of joining the Army. My eldest sister and her husband had called me to Hyderabad where he was the Military Secretary to the Governor. My sister got me a railway pass from Kurseong to Hyderabad and I was ready to go. She gave me whatever money she had, packed food for the journey and came to see me off at the tiny Railway Station of Kurseong. I boarded the *Toy Train* of Darjeeling Himalayan Railways. For a 17 year old boy just out of school and away from friends it was mixed feelings of elation, hope and fear and when I looked at the small face of my sister, standing on the platform, I felt a strong painful lump in my throat. Luckily, before tears could roll down, the train steamed off.

I had to change train at Siliguri Junction, change over through steamer in Manihari Ghat to cross Ganges River to get to Howrah. I am sure the hand of God was upon me as I befriended an Army *Havildar* (Sergeant) going on leave to Hyderabad. I told him about my NCC days and the reason of my going to Hyderabad. Thereafter he was my Godfather for the train journey. With him by my side, I had no problem reaching Howrah and getting into another train to Hyderabad. It was the month of April and the whole continent was extremely hot. I reached Hyderabad and lived with my sister and brother in law in their palatial *Raj Bhavan (Governor's House)* bungalow for a fortnight before joining the Army. My brother in law was very kind, sweet but a hard task master. The very next day he started teaching me about the army, getting me to start running to toughen myself. The heat of Hyderabad did not matter in ensuring my fitness. At the same time he gave me pocket money and pushed me to explore Hyderabad & Secunderabad cities. It was tough, hot but enjoyable to explore new places, to see *Char Minar*, the wonders of *Salarjung Museum*, walk by Tank Bund and to eat *Biryani and Brain* Curry (Veja Fry of today) floating in ghee for the first time. Not bad indeed, I still love the dish and never miss a chance to feast myself on it.

Kalimpong to Army Life Forever

Short term fun and exploration in Hyderabad came to an abrupt end. On 24th May 1963 I joined the Army as a recruit in EME (Electrical & Mechanical Engineers Corps) with the trade of Motor Vehicle (MV) Electrician. The first step was 9 months basic military training. It was a rough transition from the pleasant salubrious climate and small town school life of Kalimpong to the extreme army training in the heat and dust of Secunderabad. God has made the human body in such a beautiful manner that it has the mental and physical ability to adapt to any environment in a matter of time. The only thing needed is to make use of the mental strength that has been stored in the deep recesses of our body. Training started with a bang; physical training, running, drill, weapon handling and firing with old 303 rifles. For the first time I lived and trained with young men from all over India with a fire eating burly Sikh sergeant as the instructor. I also started learning Punjabi, Tamil languages, abuses first. I was in touch with Kunzang in Kalimpong and one fine night when I was on guard duty, a fellow recruit gave me a letter and I was thrilled to see Kunzang's handwriting on the envelope. Upon opening it I cheered alone and did a jig with my hobnailed boots on. I had passed Higher Secondary in 2nd Division. Now I was ready to take off for the officer's level exams. The Second step was technical training with the vehicles where I learnt faults and repair mechanism. By then it was 1964, Nehru died, Lal Bahadur Shastri became the Prime Minister of India and President Kennedy was shot dead. Also 5 senior generals of the Army had died in a helicopter crash.

Those were the days when our country was still under Emergency due to Chinese aggression of 1962. Training completed and I was posted out to Himachal Pradesh. As the tension with Pak was building up we moved to Kutch Bhuj and then to Rajasthan. I grabbed the opportunity to drive a Dodge Power Wagon truck all the way from Bhuj to Bikaner. Before I realised it I was in the middle of 1965 Indo Pak War where I was blessedly lucky to escape from a deadly Pakistani ambush in *Dalli Village* deep inside Pak territory. It was like "To Hell and Back". Whatever I was doing, wherever I was, even in the fog of war my aim of becoming an officer and wearing those stars on my shoulders did not waver. I had taken a unilateral decision that I would return to Kalimpong only with star on my shoulders.

I was finally selected to join the Army Cadet College in Pune in 1967. Much hard work in Academics, military drill, tactics, games, lectures, declamation contests and hosts of activities under the sun, I passed out in flying colors, receiving Chief of the Army Staff Bronze Medal, qualified to join the last bastion that was Indian Military Academy, Dehradun. I joined IMA in Jan 1969 and became the football and boxing star of the academy that got me extra marks towards the final merit.

On 14th June 1970 I was commissioned into the Assam Regiment of the Indian Army as 2nd Lieutenant. I got stars on my shoulders in an impressive piping in ceremony that included ballroom dancing and dinner at the famous Chetwood Hall of the Indian Military Academy that has the most famous motto for all officers passing out that is inscribed in the same hall:

"The safety, honor and welfare of your country come first, always and every time. The honor, welfare and comfort of the men you command come next. Your own ease, comfort and safety come last, always and every time."

Passing out of Indian Military Academy 1970 (From Left–Thakuri, Dhurba, BK Rai, Author)

I returned home to Kurseong with stars on my shoulders to the joy and pride of my family. I was not destined to visit Kalimpong even after this achievement. Duty called and I was once again baptized by fire in the bloody war of 1971 in the J&K front where I was wounded in the battlefield of Chamb.

Kalimpong after 9 Years

It was only in early 1972 during my sick leave after the war that I could see my beloved Kalimpong again. It took me 9 years of waiting and passing through a most adventurous gauntlet of life that included fighting and surviving two bloody wars. However, blessed by the soil of Kalimpong I came unscathed to be in my old hometown with proud 3 stars of captain on my shoulders.

Walking the main road of Kalimpong after 9 years, I found it narrow and small, as also other streets, Mela Ground, Town Hall, Motorstand all looked tiny to my eyes which had seen too many places for too long. Mama Himal had done very well and had erected a prestigious building on the Main Street below Girl's High School; we hugged and chatted over drinks in his first floor home. Lots of people I knew first hand seem to have grown old, balding and wearing specs. However Kalimpong was as it was, not much change. Kanchan and Novelty cinema halls were also intact. Many new faces for whom I was an alien but when walked into shops people recognised me. Sushant Jain was in Mumbai as Chemical Engineer, Surendra Pariyar in Jorhat as an Engineer with ONGC, Homenath in Bhutan as an Engineer and of Shyamal Boral had become a doctor. Pemba (Kira Kancha) had graduated to be a games teacher at Government High School and was doubling as full time musician. It was indeed a great visit but time was short and I had to be back to the unit. Thereafter I kept visiting Kalimpong off and on and every time things were changing, Kalimpong of the 50s and 60s was slowly vanishing and making way for the modern times. More vehicles and motorcycles on the road, Motor Stand was crowded and more buildings had come up everywhere. Every time I went known people were seen lesser; however my good old friend and uncle, Himal Khati has always been a constant. At one time he was operating canteen in Army Cantt, another time he had opened a fine restaurant **Chinaree** near Motor Stand. We always met and had little fun, we still do. I also meet old friend Pran Sood who has been running *Lark's*, a boutique bakery with cheese shop over the last 40 years.

Fast Forward to Kalimpong the Millennium

In June 2007, at 60 plus, after 37 military years, 5 years in the banking service and a year of roaming around the Hindu Kush Mountains, Afghanistan, Uzbekistan, Kazakhstan and places around the world, when I received an invitation to attend the centenary celebrations of my Alma Mater, SUMI Primary School. I found myself visiting the same class rooms after 50 years plus. It was the same assembly hall, where the demise of King George VI was announced by the Headmaster, saying, "the king in whose empire the sun never sets, is no more". We used to stand there bare feet and sing Christian hymns in Nepali, the meaning of which no one understood. The same class rooms where I learnt letters and words by keeping pebbles and corn on top of the alphabets written in chalk on the wooden floor by our teachers. As I walked through the same doors of our old classrooms I experienced a "major blast from the past' that I could vividly recall the events that took place in those class rooms 50 years ago. I remember how I slowly and steadily progressed from pebble (*dhoonga*) and corn (*makai)* classes to higher classes along with my steady friends like *Rishi, Pran, Gautam, Sahadev, Lasukbu, Nirmal* and so many others. On reaching class four we were officially allowed to write in "Ink" and proudly used to carry *Sulekha* Ink Bottle and a pen to school, needless to say that our hands used to be smeared with ink. On reaching class VII, like most of the boys, I started wearing shoes to the school and at class VIII I wore my first trouser. Of course, there was no school uniform; it was happiness with shorts and bare feet. I was thrilled, to once again touch the old benches and desks in the old class rooms, bearing age old marks of carved writings and sketches drawn by little hands using compass and dividers of the *tin geometry boxes* 50-60 years ago still in use. I also remembered our great masters, Rev Scott, the Principal, Longman Sir, Leela Sir, Barbes Sir, who used to hit our shinbones with military boots, Lalchand Sir who used to sell stationery to the students as we joined new classes after the winter holidays, Dhanraj sir and many others. Most of those teachers lived in nearby Mission Compound's teacher's quarters, known as *Barah Dhurah (12 roofs)*. Leonard Sir used to narrate Bible stories during our compulsory Bible classes of third period like the "Action movies" of today. I also saw the craft classrooms where we used to make ropes out of *Hathibar trees (Cactus Variety)*. The playing fields are still there where we used to run down the slopes to play volley ball and football. I set foot at the very spots where vendors used to sell snacks and sweets to us for one or two annas. At the same time, things have changed, more buildings have come up and surrounding areas of the school that was forest in our time is now covered with houses and more houses.

Epilogue

Fast forward to the present times, the saddle like ridge line on which rests Kalimpong is still standing as the saddle of a giant prehistoric fossilized horse. The layouts of the roads are same and many parts are still recognizable. The old schools, my SUMI, Girls High School in the Mission's Compound, Dr Graham's Homes sit pretty like the pommel of the saddle as ever before. Kumudini Homes in lower Bong busty, St Augustine's, St Joseph's, St Philomena's, at 8th Mile, and Government High School at 9th Mile. Dharmoday, a Buddhist Monastery cum Institution where my eldest sister used to attend BA night classes, is also there. Novelty cinema where I saw Roman Holiday and many other classic movies is still churning out movies to the present generation and the shops around that sell momo with red *chilly chatni* and *reddish aloodum* are still around but multiplied manifold but the entire area is congested with limitless parking of increasing numbers of vehicles. Kanchan Cinema Hall that screened great classics like, *The Ten*

Commandments, The Giant, Kalaa Pani, Insaniyat, sadly stands in a state of disuse, dirty and disheveled. The Glengarry of 8th Mile that used to boast one of the best rose gardens of old times although still standing, has been dwarfed to insignificance by a huge concrete monolith, Rockvale Academy. Joe's New Garage is still standing although in a state of disuse but the twists and turns of the road from 7th mile to 10th Mile are the same. The old "Thana Dara" (Police Hill) with its cottage like office is still holding ground but surrounded by extension of buildings to house the growing Police force. Across the road junction, the Boral Mansion also stands erect doing business as usual. I was so pleasantly surprised to find the old shoe maker in a small niche under the staircase of Biseseswar's building adjacent to Boral mansion. When I went to chat with the man there he turned out to be the grandson of the elderly shoemaker of our times. Very happy to see The Himalayan Store, Kalimpong's first book shop of Jain Brothers still doing business as usual under the new generation stalwart, Sandip C Jain.

Amongst friends, I am glad that Himananda, Pran, Kunzang and Dhurba are still around and we are even closer now. Just few days back, I spent a night at Pran's beautiful mansion in 8th Mile spending quality time over drinks and old times chit chat. Himananda Khati had invited me to his grand music launch on 12 Sep 2013 and he is still going strong with music, contract and family. Kunzang, now a widower, lives in his old home in Mongbul Busty after retiring as Principal of Government Higher Secondary Girl's School; Gangtok. Suren has retired as Chief Executive Engineer from ONGC and has settled in Mumbai. Sushant Jain has retired as Chemical Engineer from Corporate world and settled in Mumbai. Homenath is someone I have never met after the school but I remember him and hope to catch him before the sunset. Sahadev is leading a retired life in Sikkim after retiring from Sikkim National Transport Service, Kalzang; my roommate in Government High School was in Sikkim Politics and was a member of parliament but expired few years back. RIP old roommate. Dhurba, retired from the Army as Lt Col, dabbled in politics for a while and remains active between EX-Serviceman League, Red Cross, social work and grandchildren.

In spite of population and vehicle explosion in the concrete jungle, Kalimpong will always be beautiful. Today, tourism is booming with white water rafting in Teesta, para sailing and gliding, eco-resorts, many beautiful hotels, lodges and home stays, and the view of Kanchenjunga is as enchanting as ever. What was lost by closure of Indo-Tibet trade is being made up now by expanding tourism. Today Kalimpong is famous for nurseries of orchids, cacti, gladioli and anthurium. The mainstay of economy for the rural people is still agriculture with cash crops of rice, corn, millet, large cardamom, ginger and turmeric. The buildings, roads, schools and even some of the people of the 50s and 60s are still going strong albeit in a greyer and more wrinkled form. When I walk through the old *haat bazaar* on a Saturday, I still get the old world whiff of homemade spices mingling with fresh vegetables and dairy products from the nearby farms. I am tempted to walk into a momo shop. Gomphus restaurant and bar at the epicenter of the town since the 40s, is still the main attraction for the tourists as well as the locals. My eldest sister, *Shanti Gahatraj Ranpal,* whose name on the school honor board at Girls' High School shines even today as the Dux Prize holder of 1947, is still very fit and supple at 84. Just the other day she took a trip to Kalimpong to meet her old friend *Yankee,* also the same age, and both of them went to Tirpai Hill to meet their old teacher *Sunkeshari Gurama,* fit at 92.

Although I live in Siliguri, I keep finding excuses to visit Kalimpong often, just to feel the air of the place, walk the Main Road and catch up with old buddies Kunzang, Dhurba, Pran and Himal. Of course, I enjoy a round of golf in the most beautiful and challenging Army Golf Course in Durpin Hill. Next time I have to take the not so long trek to Kunzang's home in *Mongbul busty* and catch him sooner rather than later. Next time, need to collect my old buddies and have a drink and lunch at Gomphus.

A few days ago, I was driving to our old school, SUMI with friend Pran Sood by my side. The approach road was under repair but, encouraged by Pran, I decided to give it a try and kept driving. Looking around we were talking about our school days when I was jolted back to the present tense by the shrill and sharp voice of a small boy in SUMI uniform, ***"Grandfather, please turn back, the road is blocked"***. From 1950 we were transported back to 2014. Now we are grandfathers, cheers!

Kalimpong Army Golf Course, Durpin Hill - 2014

God Bless Kalimpong, may you remain ever green and fresh and may the fresh wind from Kanchenjunga blow through your heart and soul forever; to the time of infinity.

Book Summary

Kheopalri The Holy Lake of West Sikkim

Life form in the lake along with the bog, marsh and the jungle hill that envelope it, is slowly stirring back to life. As the morning rays of the rising sun, filtering through pine and juniper jungle, touch the highest spires of coniferous hills and start dancing on the surface of this 3500 years old lake it is time to witness the beauty. At 5 am, it is the dawn of October morning at Khecheopalri Lake in West Sikkim in India. Tucked away in a corner of the mountain; hidden by the surrounding jungle and unseen from outside, this holy water body is located at an altitude of 1700 meters (5,600 feet) as a little bowl in the middle of mountain jungle. The crisp morning air has a whiff of approaching winter and though smug and comfortable in a warm jacket, I savor the morning chill brushing through my face. Walking the short distance from the Trekker's Hut, across 100 meter long Tsozo Village market I see few doors opening and early morning smoke puffing through roof tops of few houses, perhaps brewing the morning tea for early risers. Day is just breaking and the world here is still semi dark and silent. As I cross the small clear water stream, over a culvert and continue walking along a narrow cobbled footpath that meanders into the woods I find myself entering into a different world of nature and its silence. Sound of crickets, frogs, insects and occasional chirping of birds greet me. The stone path spirals like a tunnel through juniper and pine trees across giant ferns bowing down towards the footpath as if greeting visitors to the lake. Along the slope of the path there are roughly chiseled rocks with painted prayers written in Tibetan scripts.

Trek to Sandakpu & Phalut

Sunrise in Gorkhey was another beautiful site that showcased itself by morning's first sunrays brightening the tips of the jungle of pine trees. With previous night's rain the village and the jungle around had become rain fresh. Smoke started puffing from the houses, huts and cow sheds and I could see my land lady taking fodder to her cows. Morning was further glorified by the baying of calves asking for mother's milk, goats bleating and it's little ones dancing around in their usual pranks while mother hen protectively guided her chicks to early morning worms. A lone eagle circled over the village sky in anticipation of a careless chick straying away. As I walked into the warm kitchen hot mug of tea greeted me, I picked up a chair, sat outside sipping hot tea and admiring the simple beauty of nature.

Trek to Taksang Gompa, Paro, Bhutan

At the age of 68, one needs to listen to one's body and not rush to compete with others. We pushed every step, slow and steady and continued climbing. My thigh and calf muscles started aching demanding rest. As we kept climbing my breathing became harder and started roaring into my ears. We trudged on. The mountain breeze, when it came, helped me like a breath of fresh air. A crow hovered upwind in search of a prey perhaps. The climb became grimmer as we continued to angle towards the top. My shirt, which had been soaked with sweat, now felt stiff and uncomfortable. I wiped the perspiration from my forehead that was trickling into my eyes. I glanced at the rock face towards my right and saw the holy Gompa across what looked like toy houses stuck together on the rock face with glue.

Namprikdang- Lepcha Country of Dzongu

"During such times, the air would have been frigid with cold and the travelers would have seen the puff of their breath in the red and purple afterglow of the sun. At this very place, ancestors of today's Lepchas would have made fire in their primitive ways with stones and flints, throwing slices of dried meat into the fire along with herbs, edible roots and plants for dinner. They would have relished the natural roasts with "satto" or "Champa" (powdered gram/barley/rice as "ready to eat meals") and perhaps washed it down with home brewed Chhang (country wine) from their bamboo flasks. Sitting across the campfire and talking in low whispers, those travelers of the past would have exchanged their ancient thoughts across little flames of camp fire dancing between them. Finally, tired and weary by long day's march, they would have laid over their yak skin mattress upon soft grassy ground, putting a hand between the cheek and the stone pillow below and drifted off to sleep, albeit into their ancient dreamland."

Kabul

Every morning our company staffs used to move in four vehicles in a loose convoy letting other vehicles come in between but not losing sight of each other using radios to maintain communication. One such morning as we were crossing the city limits I saw about 100 yards ahead a wheel barrow filled with goods suddenly crossing the road at a speed. There was an Afghan Army bus between my second vehicle and Praful's leading vehicle. What happened next was a blast, as suddenly the wheel barrow rammed into the side of the Afghan Army Bus and blew up. There was a huge explosion right in front of me and I could see the debris and splinters flying all over with some falling over my vehicle. My driver rammed the brakes instantly out of driver's reflex action and the vehicle came to a screeching halt few feet from the exploded bus. Before further damage and more attack could happen, purely on reflex action I told the driver to reverse the vehicle which he did but had brake again to save it from crashing against our own follow up vehicle. I knew from past experiences that in matter of minutes ISAF and Afghan Police patrols would arrive deploy and seal the area. If the attackers have not melted away there would be heavy firing and our little convoy would be right in the middle of this cauldron, justlike "Clear and Present Danger".

Kalimpong in the 50s & 60s_Life was like that

Almost every house in the villages maintained flower and vegetable gardens and we grew up on rice, corn, vegetables from own land, milk from own cows, eggs and chicken from home poultry and occasionally pork and mutton slaughtered at home or at a neighbor's house. We ate oranges, pears, figs and bananas climbing and plucking from the trees, played high jump, long jump and pole vault in our terraced fields, swam in the little ponds of clean and not so clean streams flowing by our land, we went to the jungle on picnic, cooked and ate simple rice, daal, vegetable and country chicken, obviously broiler chicken was not even born those days. Before cooking time my sisters made us run to the vegetable garden to get tomatoes, green chilies or coriander leaves fresh from the garden that is now termed organic living. My brother Bejoy and I dug and made a small pond in our land and kept small fish and shrimps, caught by us in the streams. It became tourist attraction for the visiting relatives from town.